Rowland Hill

Register This New Book

Benefits of Registering*

- ✓ FREE **replacements** of lost or damaged books
- ✓ FREE **audiobook** – *Pilgrim's Progress*, audiobook edition
- ✓ FREE information about new titles and other **freebies**

www.anekopress.com/new-book-registration

*See our website for requirements and limitations.

Rowland Hill

His Life, Anecdotes, and Pulpit Sayings

Vernon J. Charlesworth

WITH AN INTRODUCTION BY
CHARLES H. SPURGEON

We love hearing from our readers. Please contact us at www.anekopress.com/questions-comments with any questions, comments, or suggestions.

Rowland Hill
© 2022 by Aneko Press
All rights reserved. First edition 1876.
Revisions copyright 2022.

Please do not reproduce, store in a retrieval system, or transmit in any form or by any means – electronic, mechanical, photocopying, recording, or otherwise, without written permission from the publisher. Please contact us via www.AnekoPress.com for reprint and translation permissions.

Scripture quotations from The Authorized (King James) Version. Rights in the Authorized Version in the United Kingdom are vested in the Crown. Reproduced by permission of the Crown's patentee, Cambridge University Press.

Cover Designer: Jonathan Lewis
Editor: Paul Miller

Aneko Press
www.anekopress.com
Aneko Press, Life Sentence Publishing, and our logos are trademarks of
Life Sentence Publishing, Inc.
203 E. Birch Street
P.O. Box 652
Abbotsford, WI 54405

BIOGRAPHY & AUTOBIOGRAPHY / Religious

Paperback ISBN: 978-1-62245-826-4
eBook ISBN: 978-1-62245-827-1

10 9 8 7 6 5 4 3 2 1

Available where books are sold

Contents

Preface vii

Introduction ix

Part 1: Biographical Sketch
  Ch. 1: The Early Years 3
  Ch. 2: Marriage, Ordination, and Preaching 21
  Ch. 3: Inexhaustible Zeal for Christ 33
  Ch. 4: Faithful to the End 45
  Ch. 5: Testimonies to His Character and Usefulness 57

Part 2: Anecdotes
  Ch. 6: Anecdotes 71

Part 3: Pulpit Sayings and Illustrations
  Ch. 7: Pulpit Sayings and Illustrations 107

Part 4: Sermons, etc.
  Ch. 8: Christ Crucified, the Sum and Substance of the Scriptures 151
  Ch. 9: The Objective of the Christian Ministry 169
  Ch. 10: His Last Sermon at Surrey Chapel 181

Other Similar Titles 193

Servant of God, well done! They serve God well
Who serve His creatures. When the funeral bell
Tolls for the dead, there's nothing left of all
That decks the scutcheon and the velvet pall
Save this. The coronet is empty show –
The strength and loveliness are hid below.
The shifting wealth to others hath accrued.
The learning cheers not the grave's solitude.
What's done is what remains! Ah, blessed they
Who leave completed tasks of love to stay
And answer mutely for them, being dead!
Life was not purposeless, though life be fled.
    Mrs. Norton

Preface

Only a few words are necessary to introduce the following sketch and memorials of the life and ministry of Rowland Hill, and these must express the writer's obligation to the biographies written by William Jones, E. Sidney, and Mr. William Jones, formerly secretary of the Religious Tract Society. These works are only found occasionally in a secondhand bookstore, and are but little known to the present generation. I have had access to several volumes of Mr. Hill's manuscript sermons, which are still preserved in the library of Surrey Chapel. For the last fourteen years, I have enjoyed the friendship of the old members of the church, who delight to recall the memories of their early days.

It has been a work of no small difficulty to condense all the materials available to me within the limits of the present volume, and at the same time, to omit nothing necessary to enable the reader to form a proper estimate of Rowland Hill and his lifework. Rev. Hill was a gentleman by birth and education, he was a man of noble demeanor, and he was a Christian minister of a type that may be said to be apostolic.

It is hoped that this simple volume may be the means, in the hands of the Lord, of encouraging Christian workers and of suggesting methods of usefulness to others whose sphere of Christian service is not yet defined. The pulpit sayings and illustrations will furnish themes for thought in quiet hours, and may prove useful to Sunday school teachers and preachers in their ministry of love. It is sent forth with earnest prayer to this end.

Vernon J. Charlesworth
Stockwell, September 1876

Introduction

For years, Mr. Charlesworth lived in the Surrey Chapel parsonage. After having eaten, studied, and slept in rooms where Rowland Hill did the same before him, he felt he needed to write about the man's life. We do fear that like his hero, our author has a weakness for a joke, and we know that also like Rowland, he has been guilty of making hymns. We imagine that there are also other points in his character that make his subject a very pleasant one.

Pleasant or not, he has handled his pen with strength, and has produced this volume. Nothing will do except for us to write an introduction. Now I, Charles H. Spurgeon, have promised and vowed not to write any prefaces for anyone, and therefore, not even for Vernon J. Charlesworth. But we, the editor of the "Sword and Trowel," have often received contributions from the master of the Stockwell orphanage. Therefore, being very greatly indebted to him in our editorial capacity, *we* write this, and use the dignity of the plural pronoun. Take note, however, good friends, that it will be of no use to worry either *me* or *us*, for neither *I* nor *we* will write a prologue for *you*.

The majority of people who know anything about Mr. Hill associate his name with humor in the pulpit. Few judge him for using that skill, but it is seriously questioned whether anyone now living may do so without sin. It is taken for granted that wit is wicked and humor is sinful. Dullness, of course, is considered to be holy, and solemn stupidity is seen as being full of grace. We confess that we have our doubts about both propositions. If dullness were a divine power, the world would have been converted by now, for the pulpit has never been without a superabundant supply of it. If mother wit is indeed a disallowed product in the ministry, it is no small marvel that many of those who possessed it have been eminent for their usefulness in ministry.

Mr. Hill was humorous, but he was a great deal more, and those who know his lifework will not remember him as exemplifying one single quality, but as a great, good, childlike man in whom nothing was restrained, but the entirety of his redeemed nature was allowed to have harmonious play. Considering him as he was overall, we will not soon see anyone like him again. There was no dishonesty or duplicity in him. He loved his Lord and the souls of men, and he threw all his might into the pursuit of doing good. Certainly few men were ever more unselfish or less self-conscious.

People called him eccentric because they themselves were out of center. With his great heart, calm soul, wise mind, and loving nature, he had learned to wait upon his Lord, and so had found the right center and true course for his being. At first, the press had its sneers for him, but it could not lessen the respect in which he was held, and in due time it turned around and joined in the chorus of his praise. His riper years were full of honor, and like his younger days, they were full of fruit unto God.

Several writers have commemorated Rowland Hill, but their works are not now in print, resulting in the vacuum that the present volume will fill up. We see no reason why Rowland Hill and Surrey Chapel should ever be forgotten. Here is another stone for the marker that keeps his resting-place visible. The reader will be the best judge of the value of this memorial, but we have no hesitation in introducing it to him as worthy of his attention, and no fear that he will fall asleep while reading it.

Charles H. Spurgeon

Part 1
Biographical Sketch

Chapter 1

The Early Years

The name of Rowland Hill is well known throughout Christendom, but few people know much about his true character. Few men have suffered more from misrepresentation, suggested either by envy or malice, and the time has arrived to make the present generation acquainted with the prominent features of his character and the main events in his life story.

He was born on August 23, 1744, at Hawkstone, in Shropshire, England, the seat of the Hill family, and came from an honorable stock. One of his ancestors had been knighted by Henry VIII and became the first Protestant Lord Mayor of London. "Several members of the family," says Mr. Sidney, one of his biographers, "passed through the dangers of the Peninsular War, survived with honor and distinction, though not without wounds, the carnage of Waterloo, and their names will ever be conspicuous in the annals of their country's military glory."

As a boy, Rowland Hill was noteworthy for a plainspoken and generous disposition, and for the ready wit with which he delighted his friends. On one occasion, someone said to him, in the presence of his parents, "Well, Rowley, what would you like to be?" Turning toward his father, who was sitting in an armchair, he replied, "I would like to be a baronet and sit in a great chair." This ready and significant answer amused the company, and they undoubtedly concluded that he was a very promising boy. It was only a momentary ambition, however, that influenced his mind, if, indeed, the answer may not be completely attributed to his ready wit. He had probably thought no more about a profession than the boy who said he would like to be a king, and when assured that his father did not have sufficient influence to secure him a throne, promptly responded, "Then, father, I would like to be a church usher."

The coveted ease of a baronet's chair was denied to the hopeful youth, for he was destined to spend a long life of unceasing activity and toil. It is to be regretted that many young men anticipating the reward of honorable age have buried their talents, disappointed the hopes of their friends, and have gone down to an early and dishonored grave. To regard the dignity of labor as the dream of some scatterbrained old fogey who has worked like a horse in a mill, only because his neck has been kept in the collar and the crack of the whip has given a gentle reminder of the penalty of idleness, is a sure indication of disgrace and ruin. There is nothing degrading about labor, whether manual or mental, and the honest workman in any sphere is entitled to a wreath of which he may be justly proud.

With his usual concise force, Thomas Carlyle wrote, "The latest gospel in this world is, Know thy work and do it." P. J. Bailey gives expression to a similar belief, in language as powerful as it is applicable:

> We live in deeds, not years; in thoughts, not breaths;
> In feelings, not in figures on a dial.
> We should count time by heart-throbs. He most lives
> Who thinks most – feels the noblest – acts the best.

The careful reading of Dr. Isaac Watts' hymns for children awakened in young Rowland his earliest religious impressions, which were deepened by the influence of his elder brother, Richard, and his sister, Jane, who appear to have been eminent for their piety. Their concern for his spiritual welfare is seen in the solemn letters they addressed to him when he was a scholar at Eton, where he remained for about four years. For example, in a letter to Rowland dated January 7, 1764, Miss Jane Hill wrote:

> My dear Rowley,
>
> I rejoice to hear in the last letter you sent to mamma that you arrived safe at Eton and met with no inconveniences from the floods. This mark of the care of the Almighty over you may furnish you with fresh matter for praise and thankfulness. Indeed, so innumerable are the instances of divine mercy that we continually have cause to dwell on the delightful theme of praise that we trust will be our business for all eternity, joining with the heavenly host in singing hallelujahs to the God of our salvation, whose glory should be celebrated with joy and triumph by His reasonable creatures. Praise is the work of angels. Therefore, the more we abound in holy, humble, thankful, joyful praise, the more we do our Father's will as the angels do it.
>
> Oh, how dull and tasteless the pleasures of the world appear to those who have some experiential knowledge of that only true joy that comes from above, and which is centered in the Lord Jesus Christ, in whom there is fullness of joy, and at whose right hand there are pleasures for

evermore (Psalm 16:11). Christ is to the believer all that he can wish for and all that his heart can desire. He is *as the shadow of a great rock in a weary land* (Isaiah 32:2). In Him in His name, in His graces, in His comforts, and in His undertaking for poor sinners – there is that which may be their continual comfort and support. Those who are weary and heavy laden may find rest in Christ (Matthew 11:28). In Him are all the precious privileges of the new covenant, purchased by His blood and imparted by His Spirit.

How sweet are the promises in the Word of Life to a believing soul that rests upon the Lord Jesus! How sweet the knowledge of pardon, the assurances of God's love, the joys of the Holy Spirit, the hope of eternal life, and the present promises and foretastes of it to those who have their spiritual senses exercised! If the pleasures of sin are distasteful to us, divine consolations will be sweet to our tastes, *sweeter also than honey and the honeycomb* (Psalm 19:10), and we may say with the spouse, *As the apple tree among the trees of the wood, so is my beloved among the sons. I sat down under His shadow with great delight, and His fruit was sweet to my taste* (Song of Solomon 2:3).

Surely nothing on this side of heaven can be compared with the delights that accompany communion with the Redeemer and the sensible manifestations of His love. We may well desire a continuance of such blessed views and visits. But Christ will, at His good pleasure, withdraw those extraordinary communications of Himself, for He is a free agent, and His spirit, as the wind, blows when and where it desires (John 3:8), and in His pleasure it is good for us to go along with Him submissively. Our great care must be that we do nothing to cause Him to withdraw from us and to hide His face from us. We must carefully watch over our own naturally corrupt and desperately wicked hearts and suppress every thought that may grieve His good Spirit. Those who experience divine comfort should greatly fear sinning it away.

Now, my dear brother, I must conclude my letter, but not without a word or two urging you to be diligent in your school studies, and to ask you to be especially careful of reading English in your private hours. It is the sincere affection I have for you that makes me concerned for your improvement. I have often mentioned to you how disgraceful an ignorant clergyman is to the Christian religion. God knows what profession is assigned to you, but whatever it is, your unwavering care is indispensably needful, and human learning is a most desirable jewel in order to bring out the luster of those in a sanctified heart.

I do not expect you to reply to this letter, but when you write next, remember to let me know if you called on Mrs. More at Oxford. Our dear brother R. arrived well in town, as did Mr. Tudway and my sister. I hope your young friend grows in grace.

J. Hill.

At the age of eighteen, he surrendered himself to the Savior and entered upon a course of lifelong consecration to His service. The Christian religion was not a mask he wore to obtain favor with his friends, nor a creed he adopted to satisfy the craving of an active brain, but it was a life that was worked in him by the Spirit, thrilled his entire being, and constrained a wholehearted obedience to the will of God. He was thus saved from being a victim of the greatest and most deceptive fraud of the age: the profession of Christianity without knowing its power. The hypocrisy that hides the hideous deformity of a Christless character by the mask of a believable profession is one of the most abhorrent sins of which a person is capable.

Notwithstanding the intense fervor of his piety, his natural talent for wit manifested itself in his conversations with his fellow students. In a discussion as to the value of the letter *H*, some of his classmates contended that it had the full power of a letter, while others said that it was merely a breathing mark or sound and could be omitted entirely without any disadvantage. The question was not settled until Rowland remarked, "To me, the letter *H* is a most invaluable one, for if it is taken away, I will be *ill* all the days of my life."

We are not surprised to learn that he devoted himself with admirable zeal to the spiritual welfare of his companions, and that while at school he reaped the firstfruits of the abundant harvest of his future ministry. The young converts formed themselves into a society and drew up a code of rules to guide their conduct. Their goal was to promote in each other growth in grace and progress in Christian service. They recognized the importance of Christian fellowship, and they considered the mutual helpfulness of holy friendship as a gracious ordinance of God.

To young Christians especially, isolation is only another word for spiritual coldness and death. He who has commanded us not to forsake *the assembling of ourselves together* (Hebrews 10:25), and whose presence is promised wherever two or three people are gathered in His name (Matthew 18:20), has recognized the powerful inclination of the renewed heart that desires fellowship. If the unity of the church is ever manifested to the world, it will not be by the unanimous approval of believers to a formulated creed, but by their brotherly communion and fellowship in Christ.

In the year 1764, Mr. Hill moved to Cambridge and entered St. John's College in order to qualify himself for one of the livings in Norfolk, which were in the gift of the Hill family. Evangelical truth was not much valued then at the university, but he was prepared to stand by his beliefs at all costs. In a letter to Lady Glenorchy, Miss Jane Hill says, referring to her brother, "I trust that he will always stand faithful to the cause of his crucified Master, whether he is admitted as a minister of the gospel, to preach in His name, or not. Sadly, though, the world has come to such a deplorable state of apostasy that young men who are diligently devoted to the church and who live exemplary lives can hardly get their testimonials signed for orders."

The new scenes and associates of college life did not divert Rowland from his simple trust as a devout believer in, nor weaken his zeal as a devout servant of, the Lord Jesus Christ. His godly life was an eloquent rebuke of the worldly excesses of his fellow students, who made him the object of their ridicule and of their pretentious contempt. There is a dignity in the heroism of a young man, who, in steadfastness to the admonitions of conscience and the claims of God, dares to stand alone in defiance of the storm of abuse that his godly life provokes. Rowland Hill wrote, "Nobody in the college ever gave me a warm smile, except the old man who shined shoes at the gate who had the love of Christ in his heart."

It is a reason to be thankful that a great improvement has

taken place in recent years, but the reformation will not be complete until the learning of the age is brought into subjection to the authority of Christ, and a Christian character is regarded as an indispensable qualification for admission to our national colleges.

John Berridge of Everton, on hearing about the young student, wrote him a letter from Grantchester, in which he says, "If you love Jesus Christ, you will not be surprised at the familiarity shown to you by a stranger who seeks your acquaintance only out of his love to Christ and His people." Their friendship became very intimate, and Rowland Hill was laid under very considerable obligation to his eccentric counselor. The ministry of Mr. Berridge was like an oasis in the spiritual desert of his college life.[1] There can be no doubt that the young enthusiast derived help and encouragement from the example of his more experienced friend, and was encouraged to consecrate even his talent for humor to the service on which his heart was set.

Rowland's sister, in a letter addressed to him at this time, says, "My brother and I both think it is appropriate to caution you about going too frequently to Mr. Berridge, for if others find out, I do not need to tell you the storm it would raise." But Rowland was too intent upon qualifying himself for the mission of his life to be deterred by the hint of a possible storm. If he had acted upon the advice of his too prudent friends, he would have been as contemptible as the foolish, vain man who coveted the honor of a military uniform, and of whom it was said,

> But for these vile guns,
> He would himself have been a soldier.[2]

---

[1] An entire chapter is devoted to the life and ministry of John Berridge in the book *Christian Leaders of the Eighteen Century* by J. C. Ryle, available from Aneko Press.
[2] This comes from Shakespeare's play *Henry IV*.

With the most admirable devotion, Rowland Hill sought the conversion of his fellow students, and he had the joy of seeing several of them brought to a knowledge of the Savior. He also went to the villages in the vicinity of Cambridge and preached the gospel wherever he could gather an audience. He even visited the county jail and sought out the sick poor in their homes. In this way, by experience, he gained a wisdom that characterized the labors of his older years.

The storm that his sister feared soon became more threatening, for the college authorities condemned his labors as irregular, and they threatened him with immediate expulsion. Rowland appealed to Mr. George Whitefield for advice,[3] from whose reply we quote the following sentences:

About thirty-four years ago, the master of Pembroke, where I was educated, took me to task for visiting the sick and going to the prisons. . . . I would not have you give way – no, not for a moment; the storm is too great to hold long. Visiting the sick and imprisoned, and instructing the ignorant, are the very vitals of true and undefiled religion. If threatened, denied a degree, or expelled for this, it will be the best degree you can take. I have seen the dreadful consequences of giving way and looking back. Now is the time to prove that the strength of Jesus is yours. If opposition did not so much abound, your consolations would not so much abound.

With the wholehearted support of Whitefield, the approval of his own conscience, and the smile of heaven, Rowland resolved to pursue his course and to manfully brave the opposition of the college authorities. His diary contains the following record of his attempt to preach the gospel: "In a barn for the first time, with

---

3   The life and ministry of George Whitefield is also part of the book *Christian Leaders of the Eighteenth Century* that is available from Aneko Press. In addition to John Berridge and George Whitefield, the other subjects of the book are John Wesley, William Grimshaw, William Romaine, Daniel Rowlands, Henry Venn, Samuel Walker, James Hervey, Augustus Toplady, and John Fletcher.

much comfort. With God's help, if I am to live, this may not be my last barn. It is sweet to rejoice anywhere, even in a barn."

Mr. Sidney, one of Hill's biographers, said, "He was resolved to preach Christ, and it was not his natural disposition to yield to any intimidating menaces. He considered the reproach and censures cast upon him as honors of the highest order. Expulsion, or refusal of any university privilege, would have only driven him at once to other scenes of labor, and not to desponding silence and secluded inactivity."

In July of 1767, Rowland Hill returned home for the long summer vacation, and the opposition of the college authorities was now taken up by his parents. When he was an old man, he walked on the terrace of Hawkstone, the home of his youth, and said, "I have often paced this spot bitterly weeping, while by most of the inhabitants of that house I was considered a disgrace to my family."

He was sad at heart to be misunderstood, but his deepest sorrow was felt when his friends resisted his commendable attempt to benefit his fellow men. His brother Richard, with scarcely less zeal but with far more prudence, began to preach the gospel to the tenants of the estate. When Mr. Whitefield heard about this, he wrote a letter to Rowland, in which the following significant sentences occur:

Blessed, forever blessed, be the God and Father of our Lord Jesus Christ, for what He has done for your dear brother. A preaching, prison-preaching, field-preaching esquire impacts more people than all black gowns and lawn sleeves in the world.[4] And, if I am not mistaken, the great Shepherd and Bishop of souls will let the world, and His own children, too, know that He will not be dictated to in respect to men, or garments, or

---

[4] "Black gowns" refers to the ministers of the Church of England, and "lawn sleeves" refers to the bishops, whose sleeves of their robes were made of "lawn," or fine linen.

places; much less will He be confined to any order or set of men under heaven.

This was written more than a hundred years ago, but the Established Church has not yet learned the lesson, although it has been enforced by the successes of men who have never submitted to human ordination.

Returning to college in October of 1767, Rowland was more determined than ever to devote himself to the great business of soul-winning. He was wholeheartedly greeted by those to whom his ministry had been made a blessing, but there was no decrease of the opposition on the part of the authorities. His diary contains the following suggestive prayer: *Lord, grant us a deal of blessed preaching this next year.*

The same spirit that tried to hold him in check at Cambridge assumed a more aggressive form in the sister university at Oxford. No fewer than six young men were expelled simply because their zeal for the glory of God in the salvation of souls was not to be smothered by the decorum of university etiquette.

The whole situation is so instructive that we cannot fail to quote at length the judgment that was pronounced by the vice-chancellor:

I. It having appeared to me, D. Durell, Vice-Chancellor of the University of Oxford, and undoubted Visitor of St. Edmund Hall, within the said University, upon due information and examination, that James Matthews of the said Hall had been originally brought up in the trade of a weaver, and afterward followed the low occupation of keeping a tavern; that afterward, having connected himself with known Methodists, he did, without the least proficiency in school knowledge, enter St. Edmund Hall with an intent to get into holy orders; and that he still continues to be wholly illiterate, incapable of doing the required exercises of the Hall, and consequently more incapable of being qualified for holy orders, for which he had recently offered himself a candidate. Moreover, it has appeared by his own confession that he had often attended prohibited meetings held in a private house in the city of Oxford.

Therefore I, D. Durell, by virtue of my visitatorial power, and with the advice and opinion of Thomas Randolph, D.D., President of Corpus Christi College, Oxford, and Margaret Professor of Divinity in the University; of Thomas Fothergill, D.D., Provost of Queen's College; of Thomas Nowell, D.D., Principal of St. Mary's Hall, and Public Orator; and of Francis Atterbury, M.A., senior Proctor of the University, my several advisers regularly appointed on this occasion, do expel the said James Matthews from the said Hall, and do hereby pronounce him expelled.

II. It having also appeared to me that Thomas Jones of St. Edmund Hall had been brought up in the trade of a barber, which occupation he had followed very recently; that he had made only small proficiency in learning and was incapable of performing the required exercises of the said Hall; and moreover, it having appeared by his own confession that he had attended prohibited meetings in a private house in this town, and that he had himself held an assembly for public worship at Wheat Aston, in which he himself, though not in holy orders, had publicly expounded the Scriptures to a mixed congregation and offered up extemporaneous prayers.

Therefore I, D. Durell, by virtue of my visitatorial power, and with the advice and opinion of each and every one of my assessors, the pastors aforenamed, do expel the said Thomas Jones from the said Hall, and hereby pronounce him also expelled.

III. It having also appeared to me that Joseph Shipman of St. Edmund Hall had been a cloth dealer, was very illiterate, and was incapable of performing the required exercises of the said Hall. Moreover, it having appeared by his own confession that he had expounded publicly, though not in holy orders, the Holy Scriptures to a mixed congregation and offered up extemporaneous prayers. Therefore I, D. Durell, by virtue of my visitatorial power, and with the advice and opinion of each and every one of my assessors, the pastors aforenamed, do expel the said Joseph Shipman from the said Hall, and hereby pronounce him also expelled.

IV. It having also appeared to me that Erasmus Middleton of St. Edmund Hall, by his own confession, had formerly officiated in the chapel of ease belonging to the parish of Chevely, in the county of Berks, not being in holy orders; that he had been rejected from holy orders by the Bishop of Hereford for the said offense; that he was discarded by his father for being connected with the people called Methodists; and that he is still under his father's displeasure for the same. Moreover, it having appeared by credible witnesses that he is still connected with the said people and professes their doctrines – that is, that faith without works is the sole condition of salvation; that there is no necessity of works; that the immediate impulse of the Spirit is to be waited for. Therefore I, D. Durell, by virtue of my visitatorial power, and with the advice and opinion of each and every one of my assessors, the pastors aforementioned, do expel the said Erasmus Middleton from the said Hall, and hereby pronounce him also expelled.

V. It having also appeared to me that Benjamin Kay of the said Hall, by his own confession, had attended prohibited meetings in a private house in this town, where he had heard extemporaneous prayers frequently offered up by one Hewett. Moreover, it having been proved by sufficient evidence that he held Methodist principles – that is, the doctrine of absolute election, that the Spirit of God works irresistibly, and that once a child of God, always a child of God; that he had endeavored to instill the same principles in others, and exhorted them to continue steadfast in them against all opposition. Therefore I, D. Durell, by virtue of my visitatorial power, and with the advice and opinion of each and every one of my assessors, the pastors before mentioned, do expel the said Benjamin Kay from the said Hall, and hereby pronounce him also expelled.

VI. It having also appeared to me that Thomas Grove of St. Edmund Hall, although not in holy orders, had, by his own confession, recently preached in a barn to an assembly of people called Methodists, and had offered up extemporaneous prayers in that congregation. Therefore I, D. Durell, by my visitatorial power, and with the advice and opinion of each and every one of my assessors, the pastors aforenamed, do expel the said Thomas Grove from the said Hall, and hereby pronounce him also expelled.

This act of intolerance incited a fierce controversy. The cause of the expelled students was ably defended by Mr. Richard Hill, Mr. George Whitefield, and others. One of the heads of houses present at the trial cleverly observed: "As these six gentlemen were expelled for having too much religion, it would be very proper to inquire into the conduct of some who had too little." To what extent will bigotry and intolerance not go when inflamed by jealousy? Had these dignified professors never read the Savior's curse pronounced on those who offend one of His little ones (Matthew 18:6; Mark 9:42)? Were they ignorant of the rebuke that He administered to their intolerant forerunners, that *he that is not against us is for us* (Luke 9:50)?

When people cut a channel along which the river of life must flow, they would rather dam it up at the spring head than allow it to overflow the boundaries they have defined. A writer in the June 1768 *Monthly Review* congratulates the supporters of the Established Church by this "able vindication of orthodoxy," and adds, "The progress of Methodism among us has now become so considerable that it seems to be high time for rational religion and common sense to keep a good watch and defend themselves against its encroachments lest we again be overwhelmed by an inundation of pious barbarism, worse than that of those spiritual Goths and Vandals, the monks."

We will not be convicted of a breach of charity if we say that this jealousy of innovation on the part of many of the supporters of the National Church exists today, in all its intensity, and that only the strength of Nonconformity prevents its demonstration. The expulsion of these young men, with whom Rowland Hill had maintained a friendly correspondence, did not deter him from the course he was pursuing, nor weaken his attachment to the Church. We confess our utter inability to solve the mystery of how men of undoubted piety and apostolic zeal can submit to the restraints of any ecclesiastical system.

Upon completing his academic career, graduating with a Bachelor of Arts degree in 1769 and a Master of Arts three years later, Rowland Hill sought ordination. However, he said, "For visiting the sick and imprisoned, and expounding the Scriptures in private houses, I met with no less than six refusals before I gained admission into the Established Church; but, blessed be God, all this proved for the furtherance of the gospel."

He was too honest to compromise his conscience by mental reservation, and too heroic to maintain his social status and seek worldly advancement by surrendering his liberty to preach the gospel as opportunity offered. His father now reduced his annual allowance with the hope of diverting him from his erratic career and inducing obedience to order and regularity. However, with a divine commission to *go into all the world and preach the gospel to every creature* (Mark 16:15) – a commission authenticated by his great success – the opposition of friend and foe only fired his heroism and confirmed his determination to maintain his ground at all costs and in the face of any danger.

"Do not be worried about ordination," wrote Mr. Berridge to him at this time. "It will come as soon as needed; nor be concerned about anything other than to do the Lord's will and to do the Lord's work." Literally *without purse and scrip* (Mark 16:25), he went forth, journeying from place to place on a little pony, the money for the purchase of which was collected by Cornelius Winter. When he landed on his return to Bristol on one occasion, and had paid the passage across the River Severn for himself and his pony, he did not have enough money left to obtain a night's lodging, so he went on, not knowing where, hungry and exhausted.

However, his trust was in the living God, and in his deepest extremity he found adequate provision for his need. We have a rush of admiration for a young man who could thus sacrifice all for Christ and for the good of his fellow men. His diary about this time abounds with the most interesting entries, such as the following: "There was such a noise with beating of pans, shovels, etc., blowing of horns and ringing of bells, that I could hardly hear myself speak. Although we were pelted with much dirt, eggs, etc., I was enabled to preach out my sermon."

The vicar of Everton, who is worthy of being called Bishop Berridge for the encouragement and help he gave his zealous student, wrote to Hill again as follows:

I think your main work for a time will be to break up fallow ground. This suits the tone of your voice at present. God will give you other tongues when they are needed, but now He sends you out to thrash the mountains – and a glorious thrashing it is. Go forth, my dear Rowley, wherever you are invited, into the devil's territories. Carry the Redeemer's standard along with you. Blow the gospel trumpet boldly, fearing nothing yourself. If you meet with success, as I trust you will, expect clamor and threats from the world, and a little venom now and then from the children. These bitter herbs make good sauce for a young recruiting sergeant, whose heart would be lifted up with pride if it was not kept down by these pressures.

The old baronet now resolved to use further means to persuade his son Rowland to stop preaching, as Richard had already done. For this purpose, he sent Richard to search for Rowland. When he arrived at Bristol, he heard that Rowland had gone to Kingswood to preach to the miners. He immediately went to Kingswood and found Rowland surrounded by an immense multitude of these long-neglected people, who were listening with the greatest interest to the solemn appeals he made to their consciences. Rowland saw his brother, and guessing his errand, only proceeded with increased earnestness. Such was the power of his discourse that the dirty faces of the poor miners soon displayed innumerable channels of tears.

Richard was much affected by this unusual scene, and Rowland, taking advantage of his emotion, announced at the conclusion of the service, "My brother, Richard Hill, Esq., will preach here at this time tomorrow." Instead of returning in triumph with the young renegade, Richard honored this unexpected call to preach and became his brother's coworker in the very work he was commissioned to persuade him to give up.

When Rowland was again urged to seek ordination and secure a living in the Church, he said, "My desire is to win souls, not livings, and if I can secure the bees, I do not care who gets the hives."

Chapter 2

Marriage, Ordination, and Preaching

On May 23, 1773, Rowland Hill got married at Marylebone Church, and immediately afterward left town and was ordained deacon by the Bishop of Bath and Wells, who was sufficiently cautious not to impose upon the candidate "any condition whatever." He was appointed curate of the little parish of Kingston, near Taunton, in Somersetshire, where he remained about twelve months, "passing rich with forty pounds a year."[5]

His activity and zeal in carrying out his duties soon provoked opposition. It was here that he offended the farmers of his congregation by saying "they were as bad as their very pigs." As they complained that he ranted so loudly that he could be heard throughout the village, the next time he saw Hodge asleep in his pew, he exclaimed, "What! Shall we not lift up our voice like a trumpet, and cry aloud and spare not [Isaiah 58:1], when, with all our ranting, sinners can sleep and be damned under our very sermons?"

The Bishop of Carlisle now promised to admit him to priests' orders, but was commanded by an order from the Archbishop

---

5   This is a line from Oliver Goldsmith's poem "The Deserted Village."

of York "not to admit him to a further grade in the Church on account of his perpetual irregularity."

Mr. Hill's disappointment is referred to in his diary: "Without full orders, I thought it was my duty again to begin my public labors as usual." Referring to this failure, he used to say to his friends that he "ran off with only one ecclesiastical boot on."

He could now enter more fully into the work of an itinerant than before, for the fortune acquired by his marriage enabled him to bear the expenses incurred in traveling from place to place in his work of preaching the gospel. It would be impossible even to list the places he visited during this campaign, much less to record all the incidents that occurred. On one occasion, an attempt had been made to persuade him not to go to Richmond because a group of young men had rented a boat and were coming down the river with the intent of pulling him through the water. His feelings may be imagined when he was informed that the boat had capsized and that the poor misguided enemies of his ministry had all entered another world.

Mrs. Hill accompanied him in most of his preaching expeditions, and their journeys were often made less tedious by remarkable adventures. Journeying toward London on one occasion, they were stopped by a group of highwaymen. "I stood up in the carriage," he said, "and made all the outrageous noises I could think of, which frightened the fellows almost out of their wits. One of them said, 'We have stopped the devil by mistake, and had better be off.'"

The stories that refer to his treatment of his wife are pure inventions. When told of the remark he was reported to have made from the pulpit about her hat, he exclaimed to his friend, Mr. Jones, "It is an abominable untruth, derogatory to my character as a Christian and a gentleman. They would make me out to be a bear. Sir, I hope that the Christian minister in me, if not the gentleman, always prevented me from making my wife a laughingstock for the amusement of the wicked."

Nothing was more calculated to stir up his indignation than the stories that were fabricated about him. Those who were closest to him bear unequivocal testimony to the manliness of his character and the consistency of his conduct. He was scrupulously conscientious in everything, and he only violated the conventionalities of polite life when they prevented him from realizing his all-absorbing aim. When he heard of a slanderous report that the busy scandal-mongers had circulated about him, he said, "I will so live that nobody will believe it."

Many people deserve the most serious condemnation for defaming the characters of others. Few people who attain the eminence that popularity commands escape being annoyed and insulted by the venomous stings of slanderous tongues. Referring to some who had believed certain baseless stories about him, his indignation found expression in the following language: "I have humbled myself in following these gentry in language almost as low as their own; like eels, they are now at liberty to sink into their own mud and dirt as their safest place of refuge."

Hill continued his itinerant labors for a period of ten years. His ministry was attended by vast crowds. The conversions were numerous, and many of them were of a very remarkable character. In a letter to David Simpson of Macclesfield, he says:

Our greatest honor is to be sufferers for our God. No cross, no crown. For myself, I bless the Lord that I am entirely His, and I find every day that the portion of the outcast is a happy one indeed. Thousands in this city flock to hear, yet multitudes go away for lack of room. "Ecclesiastics roar," as Luther says, "like bears struck in the snout," yet they know that this is all they can do. I exceedingly long for your share of humility and restraint, yet a little courage to face the devil may not be inappropriate. The Lord knows how difficult it is to keep measures with the wretched and much-to-be-pitied church governors at the present day.

Rowland Hill thus proved himself to be a worthy member of the Methodist party, which began with the labors of Whitefield and the Wesleys. He traversed the three kingdoms preaching the gospel, and he found a joy in his labors that more than compensated for the sorrow he endured from family and priestly persecutions. Hampstead Heath and London Fields in the north, and Kennington Common and Blackheath in the south, were his favorite places for open-air services in London. As he was preaching on Hampstead Heath on one occasion, it began to rain, and the crowd became somewhat restless. He very deliberately put on his hat and said, "Excuse my hat, friends, but do not let the rain alarm us so much. What would the condemned souls in Tophet's parched pit give for a single drop of this refreshing rain that falls upon our delightful land and makes our dry fields fruitful?"

At a place near Redruth, in Cornwall, there is an amphitheater formed by a mine that fell in. Here John Wesley and John Nelson preached to large congregations, and meeting with no one to show them hospitality, they slept on the ground for lack of lodging and picked blackberries to satisfy their hunger. It was also here that Rowland Hill proclaimed the message of mercy to listening thousands.

At another time, preaching in a field near Wrexham, one of those crazy incidents occurred that are fatal to the solemnity and composure of a preacher, and that threaten to imperil the success of the sermon. Near the spot was a field with a large tenterhook frame (used to stretch and dry cloth) on which a fine kind of thread, or yarn, was exposed to the air. Several women who were taking care of it saw a number of people assembling together and decided to stop their work for a little while. The gate of the field had been left open, and several large pigs walked in. In a few moments, the intruders got the iron that was pierced through their snouts entangled in the twine, and the more they shook, the more they found themselves imprisoned. The loud cries of the pigs alarmed the women, who soon found out the mischief that had been done. They ran to the spot, and a general pursuit took place. Mr. Hill, while preaching, observed several of the women falling upon the poor animals, turning them on their backs, and then trying to unravel the twine from their heads. This produced considerable amusement, and for a time interfered with the service.

Acknowledgments of good received were often sent in, as well as requests for special prayer. As his preaching engagements necessarily caused him to travel extensively in various directions, he constantly availed himself of the advantage of his carriage and horses. On one occasion, a rigid Sabbatarian (one who strictly observes the Sabbath, or Lord's Day, as if under the Law) resorted to a very questionable method to rebuke Mr. Hill, and sent in a request for prayer. Mr. Hill took it and began to read it: "The prayers of this congregation are desired..." Having read that much, he exclaimed, "Umph! 'for...' – umph! Well, I suppose I must finish what I have begun – 'for Rowland Hill, that he will not go riding about in his carriage on a Sunday!'" Any ordinary man would have been disconcerted, but he looked up very calmly and said, "If the writer of this piece of folly and impertinence is in the congregation, and will go into the vestry after the service and let me put a saddle on his back, I will ride him home instead of going in my carriage." When his nephew, Mr. Sidney, asked him if this story were true, he replied, "Yes, that it is, true enough. You know I could not call him a donkey in plain terms."

Holding Calvinistic views, Rowland Hill took part with Augustus Toplady against John Fletcher and John Wesley in the controversy then raging. It is to be greatly regretted that time and temper should have been sacrificed to the purposes of controversy by such honorable men, who were agreed on fundamental doctrines, when all their energies were required to fight the common battle against sin. However, with all his Calvinism, Mr. Hill preached a full and free gospel, and he adorned the doctrines he professed by the virtues of a holy character.

Of course, he was accused of being inconsistent, but is it not the truest consistency to embrace the entirety of divine revelation without attempting to reconcile the seeming difference between the universality of the gospel call and its limited application? Election and free agency appear to us as two parallel lines, but as they have an inclination toward each other, which we, perhaps, cannot detect, they must meet in the throne of the Eternal.

Wesley and Fletcher were at the end of one line, preaching salvation by grace, but contemplating man as a free agent. Hill and Toplady were at the end of the other, preaching the same gospel, but regarding God as Sovereign. If they had looked above the clouds of controversy, they would have been assured that the converging lines would be seen to meet in the perfected scheme of divine redemption. If Rowland Hill had followed the counsel of his eminent prototype, John Berridge, he would have spared himself the sorrow that the controversy involved. "My dear friend," Berridge wrote, "keep out of all controversy, and wage no war but with the devil."

The sincerity of those men on both sides is most apparent, and they all lived to regret, we believe, the unchristian frame of mind into which they were sometimes betrayed. We do not apologize for either party, but rather prefer to draw the veil of charity over the most painful episode in the histories of some of the most sincere men who have labored in the gospel of Jesus Christ. Rowland Hill was as severely blamed by the high doctrinalists for not preaching to the elect only, as he was by the Arminians for preaching too much Calvinism. When someone complained that he did not preach to the elect only, he said, "I don't know them, or I would preach to them. Have the goodness to mark them with a bit of chalk, and then I'll talk to them!"

Notwithstanding his love of itinerant preaching, Mr. Hill at times felt the advantage that would be gained from a regular sphere of labor. He had originally contemplated exercising his ministry within the confines of the Established Church, but now he felt he was destined to occupy a wider field of service.

The south of London, which shared only a few of the advantages of the north, was regarded by Rowland Hill as presenting a fine sphere of labor. During the Gordon riots in 1780, he frequently addressed as many as twenty thousand people in St. George's Fields. The principal chapels in the north were the Tabernacle in Moorfields, built for Mr. Whitefield, and opened in 1753; the Tabernacle in Tottenham Court Road, opened in 1756 (Whitefield's funeral sermon was preached here in 1770 by John Wesley); Mr. Wesley's Chapel in the City Road, opened in 1777; and Spa Fields Chapel, originally built as a place of amusement, and ultimately purchased by the Countess of Huntingdon in 1779. The pulpits of these chapels, with the exception of John Wesley's, were open to Mr. Hill, and on the death of Mr. Whitefield in 1770, he was spoken of as his probable successor. But while Mr. Hill had access to many of the Dissenting pulpits, he was denied the same privilege in the chapels belonging to the Countess of Huntingdon. Although she rejoiced in the success of his labors, she refused to allow him to use her chapels, and Mr. Hill is mentioned in her will as one of the men who were not to be appointed or permitted to preach in any of her chapels.

Soon after the Gordon riots, the earnestness of Mr. Hill in proclaiming the gospel in the south of London convinced some people of influence to come forward and propose the construction of a large chapel in that particular neighborhood where Mr. Hill could labor regularly, unbound by ecclesiastical restraints. The site was chosen in the Blackfriars Road, and the first stone of the building, known throughout the religious world as "Surrey Chapel," was laid on June 24, 1782, and opened on Whit Sunday, June 8, 1783. Mr. Hill preached from the text, *We preach Christ crucified* (1 Corinthians 1:23).

Mr. Berridge, who happened to be in London at the time when the first meeting was held to determine the site for Surrey Chapel, wrote to the Countess of Huntingdon:

I am persuaded that your ladyship will rejoice that dear Rowley is going, with the Lord's help, to erect a standard for the gospel in the very middle of the devil's territories in London. What a bellowing and a clamor the old enemy will make at this fresh invasion of his kingdom! He may storm and rage and persecute, but Christ's cause must and will prevail over every opposition men or devils can raise. A meeting has been held, and I am told the place fixed upon is one of the worst spots in London, the very paradise of devils. This much is satisfactory. It is fine soil for plowing and sowing! In time, my lady, we will hear of the reaping time, the harvest, and the harvest home. How glorious will be the triumphs of the gospel in that place! I am now looking every day to hear that the foundation stone has been laid, and the King of Zion consecrating the spot by the conversion of souls to Himself. I do not need to remind your to pour forth a volley of prayers for the success of this sanctuary.

In replying, the Countess provided the following testimony:

I, who have known Mr. Hill from the time he first set out in ministry, can testify that no man ever engaged with more heartfelt earnestness in bringing captives from the strongholds of Satan into the glorious liberty of the gospel of our Emmanuel, and it will require all the energies of his zealous and enterprising spirit to erect the standard of the cross in that part of London, where ignorance and depravity prevail to such a dreadful degree. Though I have seen sufficient cause to exclude him from serving in my chapels for the present, yet I cordially rejoice in the success that has attended his faithful labors.

The appointment of Rowland Hill as minister of Surrey Chapel was confirmed by the trustees, in whom the choice of a minister was invested. His evangelistic labors were not restricted, however, when he assumed the pastoral office, for he claimed the liberty of being absent for six months of the year so that he could evangelize throughout the country. He facetiously described himself as "the rector of Surrey Chapel, vicar of Wotton-under-edge, and curate of all the fields and lanes throughout England and Wales." The desire he expressed in the opening sentences of the first sermon he preached has become an answered prayer: "that the worship of God in Surrey Chapel might prove the beginning of happy days to thousands who were already born of God, and the cause of future joy to tens of thousands who were then dead in trespasses and sins."

Wotton-under-edge in Gloucestershire, where Mr. Hill had already built a house and chapel, and where he ministered during a portion of the time he was absent from London, is described by his nephew, Mr. Sidney:

Opposite the house is the most perfect amphitheater of hill, three parts of which is clothed with a hanging wood of exquisite variety of foliage, enclosing a dale of the richest fertility. The summit of a hill on the left of the house commands a landscape on which Nature has lavished her choicest attractions. The Welsh mountains, the Malvern hills, the rich vale of Berkley, the broad course of the silvery and majestic Severn, and a foreground of grassy knolls and hanging woods form the principal features of a scene in which all are blended in the loveliest harmony and proportions. In front of the house, a rocky path winding through a sloping wood of beech breaks it, with its white and narrow streaks, into clusters of great beauty and variety. On the Lord's Day, this road is teemed with human beings coming from the lovely glens around to hear the Word of Life from the lips of their beloved minister.

Robert Hall visited his friend in this rural retreat, and remarked to him, "Sir, it is the most paradisaical spot I was ever in."

In selecting an assistant for the chapel at Wotton, toward the close of his life, Mr. Hill described the man on whom his heart was set, and the preacher the people wanted to hear. He said, "They don't want a dictionary preacher, for they cannot understand him; nor a showy preacher, for they will despise him; nor a bad-tempered preacher, for he will divide them; but a man with a good loud voice, a disposition to be taught, with brains in his head and grace in his heart." For fifteen years, Theophilus Jones was a faithful servant of the Church, a successful soul winner, and an acceptable supply at Surrey Chapel. His voice was so powerful that he could be heard some distance from the chapel on a summer's evening when the windows were open.

The following letter to him from the pen of Rowland Hill describes him:

> If you were to continue as the same plain, bawling Welshman you are now, in your present situation, I might tell you to continue as you are. Never mind breaking grammar if the Lord enables you to break hearts and bring souls to Christ; but if you could acquire a little more culture, without losing any of your zeal and holy simplicity of heart, your usefulness might be more extended. I would not give you a single sixpence to have your tongue dressed at any of our modern academies. They are, in general, sad

soul-starvation places. Only take the hint, and work on, and blunder on as hard and as fast as you can.

The chapel at Wotton in which Mr. Hill preached was pulled down a few years ago, and a structure in accordance with modern ideas was erected on its site.

It may be regretted by some that Surrey Chapel was not affiliated with either of the existing denominations. Undoubtedly, Mr. Hill thought it would have been opposed to the unity for which he contended to make it a part of any denominational system. However, he sought to cultivate friendly relations with all the denominations without being absorbed by any of them. It was his proud boast that evangelical ministers of all communions were free to preach in his pulpit. Venn, Scott, Berridge, and Pentycross were some of the eminent Episcopalians who preached at Surrey Chapel during the earlier years of its history; and Jay, Sibree, Bull, and James were as frequently found in the list of preachers, representing the Dissenters.

Rowland adopted the liturgical service of the Church of England from the beginning. As an independent church, it was free to adopt this form of service, but whether the advantages justified doing so leaves some room for doubt. Mr. Hill's salary at Surrey Chapel never exceeded £300 per year, and out of this sum he paid those who preached during his summer vacation. He consecrated the entire fortune he acquired upon the death of his father to the work in which he was engaged, and found in the sacrifice a joy to which those who only live to gain are total strangers. It was a common saying with him, "The best of living is to live for others."

We get a glimpse of Rowland Hill's theory of church government in his *Journal of a Tour through the North of England and Parts of Scotland,* in which he says:

I like the idea of minister and elders. The elders, like

councilmen of a city, should be representatives of the younger members of the church, whose general support and approval should at all times be sought. Government should be a delegated business, and a few well-chosen people always accomplish the best work. These elders should attend to the arrangement of the congregation, while the people at large should be heard on every proper occasion. This modified independency is far more conducive to order and good government than the system that concedes the power to the entire church and demands that the vote of the church be taken upon every question of petty detail.

From its commencement, Surrey Chapel has been the center of a system of benevolent societies designed to reach the various classes of the community. The Benevolent Society, founded in the year 1784, has for its object the relief and instruction of the sick poor in their own houses by the active members of the church. The first Sunday school in the metropolis was established by Rowland Hill, soon after the opening of Surrey Chapel. In 1799, three or four other schools, which had been established in various parts of Southwark, mainly through the zeal of Thomas Cranfield, a person humble in life, but endowed with strong faith, were incorporated with Mr. Hill's school at Surrey Chapel under the title of the Southwark Sunday School Society. The School of Industry, for the clothing and education of twenty-four girls, and the almshouses for as many poor women, are two of the most valuable institutions in connection with Surrey Chapel.

Chapter 3

Inexhaustible Zeal for Christ

The observation is sometimes made that Rowland Hill could not have succeeded in the present day. We object. We believe he would have been successful in any age, for he possessed the attribute of greatness, and he wisely adapted himself to the circumstances of the sphere in which his lot was cast and the nature of the commission he was called to fulfil. Thomas Carlyle very truly says, "The hero can be poet, prophet, king, priest, or what you will, according to the world he finds himself born into. I confess, I have no notion of a truly great man that could not be all sorts of men." It is utterly impossible to declare with any degree of certainty the success or failure of a man in any given age or sphere.

Rowland Hill was called to be a preacher when evangelical religion was not much valued by the ordained ministers of the national church. Many of them were dreadfully negligent in their sacred duties, and the immorality of others was a standing disgrace. The people were kept in complete ignorance of the vital doctrines of Christianity, and their conduct was seldom influenced for good by the teachers appointed by the State. Their social condition was deplorable to the last degree.

A man of simple faith and genuine piety, despising a show of religion on the one hand, and guarding against that questionable and weak pietism on the other that avoids boldly affirming and following Christ, Mr. Hill found the fields white unto harvest (John 4:35), and he brought all the energies of his redeemed manhood to bear upon the work to which he had received an indisputable call. He was a living man, and living men must speak. He was intensely earnest, and earnestness is never silent. From the moment of his conversion to the latest hour of his life, he despised that cowardly reluctance by which many Christians, otherwise honorable, hide their light under a bushel and weaken the testimony to the grace of God. It is not that he paraded his piety by pharisaic boasting or the pompous use of sanctimonious language, for the language of his lips had complete interaction with the emotions of his heart, and the testimony of his ministry was the faithful evidence of his saintly character.

His views of truth were eminently evangelical and decidedly Calvinistic. The narrowness of the Bible was sufficiently broad for the compass of his creed, and he preferred the simplest utterance of inspired revelation to the profoundest speculations of an unsanctified philosophy. He was intolerant of that rationalistic spirit that has developed so rapidly lately, and by which the gospel is obscured and the truth of God is made *of none effect* (Mark 7:13). The substance of his preaching was expressed by the alliterative trinity:

- Ruin by the fall,
- Redemption by the cross of Christ, and
- Regeneration by the Holy Spirit.

When examining a young man for the ministry, he said, "Well, the gospel is a good milk cow; she gives plenty of milk. I never write my sermons. I first give a pull at justification, then a plug at adoption, and afterward, a bit at sanctification; and so, in one way or the other, I fill my pail with the gospel milk."

The success of his ministry is sufficient evidence that this kind of preaching enjoys divine approval. Ministers may moralize until they are out of words, but moral reasoning never saved a soul from death. They may philosophize until the "crack of doom,"[6] but theory never won a soul to Christ. The people may be charmed into professing religion by the subtle sophistries of a rationalistic theology, the fascinating enchantments of an ornate ritual, and the beauties of an artistic symbolism – but a profession is of no value unless it represents one's inner life. *If any man have not the Spirit of Christ, he is none of His* (Romans 8:9).

Rowland Hill was an extemporaneous preacher, and he delivered, on average, three hundred and fifty sermons a year for a period of sixty-six years. In speaking of the custom of reading sermons, he once said, "If a minister, after having properly considered the leading truth of his text, would only dare, under the divine blessing, to apply the subject from the natural ability that God may have given him, he would find his heart enlivened by the subject, and preaching would soon be his daily delight."

Undoubtedly, his sermons often lacked method, but this must not be attributed to his inability to arrange his thoughts in logical order. He knew that no sinner was ever savingly impressed by a sermon when considered as a whole, but by some powerful thought or appropriate appeal, likely not planned by the preacher and not forming a necessary part of the discourse.

"Some of you may think," he said to his audience at Surrey Chapel on one occasion, "that I am preaching a wandering sermon; but oh, if I am able to reach the heart of a poor wandering sinner, I'm sure you'll forgive me." He went on to say, "Sinner,

---

6   The "crack of doom" is a phrase from Shakespeare's *Macbeth* and refers to the end of the world, or judgment day.

you may wander from Christ, but we will roam after you and try to bring you back into His fold." At the moment these words were being uttered, a pickpocket entered the chapel, and his conversion was traced to the impression then produced. When one person in his congregation said to him, "Mr. Hill, you have taken us from Dan to Beersheba in your sermon today," he very sincerely replied, "Never mind, my friend; it is all holy ground."

There is no doubt that Mr. Hill described himself in his *Village Dialogues* when depicting Mr. Lovegood:

If by the energy of his imagination he excited a smile of approval without the least degree of levity, he knew how very soon afterward to excite a tear. His preaching was, at times, brilliant like the sun, and even if intervening clouds intercepted its bright rays, yet still the warmth was felt and its fertilizing effects were evident. His sentiments were elevated and pure. If he descended, it was like the swallow, just to dip the tip of his wing in the stream and again ascend. After he had taken his text, he would stick to it for a time and give it a just and correct interpretation, though afterward, from the warmth and animated frame of his mind, he would branch out so as to surprise his hearers by a brilliancy of thought peculiar to himself. His more austere hearers would find fault with him for his eccentricities and call him a wandering preacher, though still he was correct in his divinity and well-intentioned in his design, and in all his wanderings he was always sure to remain upon holy ground.

The simplicity of his faith and the sincerity of his purpose were sustained by prayer. He consecrated all his talents at the throne of grace, and he maintained the strength of his spiritual life by prayer. It was a very important factor in the success of his noble lifework, for it is the secret of all true success in the work and warfare of the kingdom of God. The men who have revolutionized society by their heroic deeds in the cause of God have been mighty through the inspiration of prayer. Paul and Luther, Wesley and Whitefield, and the noble army of martyrs became bold to dare and strong to do because they were men of prayer.

> More things are wrought by prayer
> Than this world dreams of. Wherefore, let thy voice
> Rise like a fountain for me night and day.
> For what are men better than sheep or goats
> That nourish a blind life within the brain,
> If, knowing God, they lift not hands of prayer
> Both for themselves and those who call them friend?
> For so the whole round earth is every way
> Bound by gold chains about the feet of God.[7]

Rowland Hill became so familiar with the art of prayer that he was only conscious of a few intervals during the day when his heart was not drawn up to God in prayer. He said on one occasion, "I like short, direct prayer: it reaches heaven before the devil can get a shot at it." He was a living embodiment of James Montgomery's charming hymn, and had indeed proved that "prayer is the Christian's vital breath."[8]

Sustained by prayer, he was wholehearted in his consecration to the service of Christ and untiring in his labors for the good of his fellow men. Surrey Chapel was the center of his parish, but its boundaries were the coastlines of the United Kingdom. He was not like a parish water cart that spends its time within well-defined limits, but was more like the aerial reservoirs, the clouds, that recognize no restrictive boundary in their beneficial

---

[7] This is from "The Passing of Arthur, or "Morte d'Arthur," in *Idylls of the King* by Alfred Lord Tennyson.

[8] This line is from the hymn by James Montgomery (1771-1854) that begins with "Prayer is the soul's sincere desire."

mission. Rowland Hill used to say, "I always thought that in preaching throughout England, Scotland, Ireland, and Wales, I stuck close to my parish."

Charged with a divine commission, he went everywhere preaching the gospel (Acts 8:4). He did not need any ecclesiastical authorization for the limits of his ministry when his Master had specified *all the world* (Mark 16:15) as his sphere of service. The system that confines the preaching of the gospel to consecrated walls, and sacrifices usefulness to decorum, is not according to the mind of Christ.

His soul was fired with zeal, and he brought his natural talent for wit and humor to bear upon his work. He was no clown in the pulpit, however, nor did he indulge in coarse and random jokes.

"He was serious in a serious cause," and he simply supported his heavy artillery of truth with the light musketry of his wit. A close friend of William Cowper, he felt as Cowper did when he wrote:

> 'Tis pitiful
> To court a grin when you should woo a soul;
> To break a jest when pity should inspire
> Pathetic exhortation; and to address
> The skittish fancy with facetious tales
> When sent with God's commission to the heart.[9]

It is true that he resorted to many unusual methods to gain people's attention, but it was done with such expert skill that they never diverted attention from his great purpose. He once began a sermon by shouting, "Matches! Matches! Matches!" He then went on to say, "You wonder at my text, but this morning, while I was engaged in my study, the devil whispered to me,

---

9   This is from *The Task* by William Cowper (1731-1800).

'Ah, Rowland, your zeal is indeed noble, and how tirelessly you labor for the salvation of souls.' At that very moment a man passed under my window, calling out, "Matches" very loudly, and my conscience said to me, 'Rowland, you never labored to save souls with half the zeal this man does to sell matches.'" With this introduction, he proceeded with his sermon, and the attention, gained at the beginning, was held to the close.

He always preached with the power of the Holy Spirit and a passion that moved the hearts of the people, and in the pulpit his influence was impressive. The most hardened sinner trembled under his preaching when he dealt with the stern realities of the world to come, and those ashamed of and remorseful for their sin were won by his touching appeals when he spoke of the love of Jesus. Dramatist and politician Richard Sheridan used to say, "I go to hear Rowland Hill because his ideas come red-hot from the heart;" and it was the opinion of Robert Hall that "no man has ever drawn, since the days of our Savior, such sublime images from nature."

In writing to his nephew, Rowland Hill said, "It is better to feed the appetite of the hungry than to tickle the fancies of the whimsical. Preachers of this breed are soon apt to preach themselves out of breath and come to nothing. May you and I never be the retailers of such whipped-cream divinity. It is better to run a restaurant to satisfy the hungering appetite than to run a bakery to indulge the unwholesome appetite of the dainty. Good, brown-bread preaching is the best after all."

Mr. Hill's energies were not exhausted by his preaching, nor were the desires of his heart satisfied by the gracious results that followed. Therefore, we find him honorably connected with the formation of the principal societies that were called into existence by the revived activities of the churches. His interest in the London Missionary Society, of which he was one of the founders, was maintained until the end of his life. On one occasion, he objected with considerable severity against those finely dressed people who spend all their money on their clothing while giving nothing but dimes and nickels for the cause of the perishing heathen.

The Religious Tract Society was formed on May 9, 1799. The first meeting was held in the vestry of Surrey Chapel. The preliminary measures for promoting the formation of the British and Foreign Bible Society were determined in the committee of the Religious Tract Society in 1802. Thus we see how one good work that is efficiently maintained leads to the establishment of others. Mr. Hill was a loyal friend and supporter of the Society from its commencement to the end of his life.

In his response to a letter from Mr. William Jones, requesting him to act as chairman of a meeting, Mr. Hill wrote the following characteristic reply:

Wotton, September 20, 1826

My Dear Friend,

An old man in the 83rd year of his age ought to be a little frugal with his remaining strength. You will say that no bodily strength can be needed to sit quietly in a chair at a public meeting. That is true, but no small degree of patience is needed for the poor chairman to sit it out for at least three hours to hear many different tiresome, long speeches (if they are not all of the same kind) without any remedy or compensation, while being extremely restless and spending more than half the time yawning and watching the clock. In most of these public meetings, I have been tired enough to sleep before they have been half over, and have been obliged to wander off with the remains of my patience and leave the finishing to others, while nothing but a short speech might have been expected from me.

In the way in which too many of these kinds of meetings are now conducted, I have my fears that many good causes are injured by the means adopted for their support. Though some may be gratified by what may be said to the point, yet, oh, the dullness, the unnecessary long-windedness, the conceit, the verbosity, etc., etc., of others!

In short, few know how to be concise, short, and sweet. And as I find it very difficult to be concise and sweet, my refuge at all times is to be short.

Therefore, pity a poor old man, and do not let him be sentenced to suffer such a type of excruciating punishment, and see if you cannot persuade some other good-tempered sinner to suffer in his place.

Yours very sincerely and affectionately,

Rowland Hill

Mr. Hill's entire career is a splendid protest against the partisanship by which too many honorable Christians have restricted their usefulness and brought discredit upon the cause of God. When Dr. Bogue, in the course of a sermon, referred to the universality of the Missionary Society at its formation, he exclaimed, "We are called upon this evening to the funeral of sectarianism, and I hope it will be buried so deep as never to rise again."

Mr. Hill wrote the following epitaph, but unfortunately it was too soon, for the monster still lives:

> Here lies old Bigotry, abhorred
> By all who love our common Lord;
> No more his influence shall prove
> The torment of the sons of Love.
>
> We celebrate with holy mirth
> This monster's death, of hellish birth;
> Ne'er may his hateful influence rise
> Again to blast our sacred joys.
>
> Glory to God, we now are one,
> United to our Head alone;
> With undivided hearts we praise
> Our God, for His uniting grace.
>
> Let names, and sects, and parties fall,
> Let Jesus Christ be all in all;
> Thus, like Thy saints above, shall we
> Be one with each, as one with Thee.

He was in full sympathy with the Christian desire of pastor and hymnwriter Benjamin Beddome (1717-1795), who wrote:

> Let party names no more
>   The Christian world o'erspread;
> Gentile and Jew, and bond and free,
>   Are one in Christ, their Head.
>
> Among the saints on earth
>   Let mutual love be found,

> Heirs of the same inheritance,
>   With mutual blessings crowned.
>
> Let bitterness and wrath
>   Be banished far away;
> Those should in strictest friendship dwell
>   Who the same Lord obey.
>
> Thus will the church below
>   Resemble that above,
> Where streams of pleasure ever flow,
>   And every heart is love.

He was no advocate of uniformity, however. His early experience had taught him that it was impossible to attain it, and he had learned that the attempt to enforce it could only lead to tyranny and injustice. With regard to the walls that separated the different denominations, he said, "I do not want such partitions destroyed, but only lowered a little so that we may shake hands a little easier over them."

He was not, though, willing to compromise truth to secure friendly relations with his fellow Christians. His jealousy for the truth brought him into conflict with many who could not agree with his views. William Huntington frequently felt the lash that Mr. Hill administered to those whose doctrines leaned toward Antinomianism. The writer of the life of Huntington says that Mr. Hill was the first person who called him an Antinomian, and that he often called him his godfather for giving him the name. Hill's opposition to the school of theology that Mr. Huntington supported was due to his conviction that such teaching was intended to weaken the divine precepts in their application to the conduct of Christians, and he was not, therefore, going to endanger his own case by allowing in himself what he condemned in others.

He said from the pulpit, "I once met with an Antinomian professor, in Gloucestershire, who told me that he will never doubt his salvation anymore. I said to him, 'If you are done doubting for yourself, allow me to doubt for you.' We do not doubt for those who want more grace and desire to get nearer to God, but we doubt for those who live how they want regardless of the precepts of the Bible."

In one of his sermons, he made this remark, "I would rather see the devil in the pulpit than an Antinomian." One of the last remarks he made on his dying bed was, "The greatest curse that ever entered the church of God is dirty Antinomianism."

Few men were more generous than Mr. Hill in giving away their possessions. It is said that his wife had to frequently urge a gentle protest in their early days, or he would have given his last dime to some needy person. He could always refer to his own example when advocating for others to give to a cause. This gave him an advantage, also, in dealing with those who, while admitting that *it is more blessed to give than to receive* (Acts 20:35), had failed to test its truth by personal experience. He was certainly not a miser, and spoke against those who were.

In denouncing debt as unworthy of a Christian, he said, "I never pay my debts, and for the best of all reasons – I never have any debts to pay." On being asked at a public meeting whether anyone in debt should give to the collection, he replied, "Certainly not;" and then, with a merry twinkle of his eye, he informed the audience that he would "stand at the door and notice who passed the plate without giving."

Chapter 4

Faithful to the End

As an author, Mr. Hill rendered valuable service to the cause of truth. His *Village Dialogues* is still popular in many parts of the country, and it provides a fair example of the way in which many of the clergy of that day carried out their sacred functions. However, most of his works were of a controversial nature, and were not designed to survive the necessities of the hour. In 1803 he published a pamphlet entitled "Spiritual Characteristics: Represented in an Account of a Most Curious Sale of Curates by Public Auction, Who Were to Be Disposed of in Consequence of the Clergy Residence Act." This was a clever satire on the clergy of the day, and it called down a storm of abuse upon the author. However, not wanting to imperil his usefulness, he withdrew it from circulation. Another of his writings, his "Warning to Professors on the Nature and Tendency of Public Amusements," was demanded by the lax morality of the age.

His poetical talents were admirable, too, as his *Divine Hymns for Children* and various compositions fully prove. We include a sample here:

Dear Friend of friendless sinners, hear,
    And magnify Thy grace divine;
Pardon a worm that would draw near,
    That would his heart to Thee resign:
A worm by self and sin oppressed,
    That pants to reach Thy promised rest.

With holy fear and reverent love,
    I long to lie beneath Thy throne:
I long in Thee to live and move,
    And charge myself on Thee alone:
Teach me to lean upon Thy breast.
    To find in Thee the promised rest.

Thou say'st Thou wilt Thy servants keep
    In perfect peace, whose minds shall be,
Like newborn babes or helpless sheep,
    Completely stayed, dear Lord, on Thee:
How calm their state, how truly blest.
    Who trust on Thee, the promised rest.

Take me, my Savior, as Thine own,
    And vindicate my righteous cause;
Be Thou my portion, Lord, alone,
    And bend me to obey Thy laws:
In Thy dear arms of Love caressed,
    Give me to find Thy promised rest.

Bid the tempestuous rage of sin,
    With all its wrathful fury, die;
Let the Redeemer dwell within,
    And turn my sorrows into joy;
Oh, may my heart, by Thee possessed,
    Know Thee to be my promised rest.

The following is from his *Divine Hymns for Children: Designed as an Appendix to Dr. Watts's Divine Songs*:

> Dear Jesus, let an infant claim
>   The favor to adore Thy name:
> Thou wast so weak, that babes might be
>   Encouraged to draw near to Thee.
>
> My gracious Savior, I believe
>   Thou canst a little child receive;
> Thy tender love for us is free,
>   And why not love poor sinful me?
>
> Then to a child, dear Lord, impart
>   An humble, meek, and lowly heart:
> Oh, cleanse me by Thy precious blood,
>   And fill me with the love of God.
>
> Tho' oft I sin, yet save me still,
>   And make me love Thy sacred will;
> Each day prepare me by Thy grace
>   To meet Thee and behold Thy face.

These hymns are decent examples of both the style and doctrines of his poetical compositions.

His letters exhibit all the characteristics that made him famous. We include the following examples:

Letter to Mr. Bull

My Dear Brother Bull,

At last the famous publication is out (a hymnbook published by Mr. Hill: Cowper, Bull, Hill, & Co.). The paper is so cheap, the printing so bad, and the typographical blunders so prominent that I have not attempted to advertise the book. My printer is a poor man, and it is a charity to employ him, but he is the biggest blunderer in all the world, myself not excepted. I intend, if I can, not to advertise it until the next edition, and that will be more correct. Mr. Cowper will find all his thoughtful amendments strictly attended to. The omissions are so small that I think he himself would judge them scarcely worth an apology. I think you know them all. I have mentioned the corrector's name in the preface, just as you have directed. While I was at Clapham, I heard that you are to come to London on Good Friday. Therefore, I told Mr. Thornton that I would ask you to come to our house on Good Thursday, and that if you preached a good sermon, I would send you on Good Friday afternoon to good Mr. Thornton's, with a good number of thanks for your good services. My good wife also promises you a good supper, and a good pipe, and a good bed, provided you give us a little notice that we are to expect your good company. So, wishing you a good night, as it is a good while past eleven o'clock, I remain, though after a poor rate,

Your good friend and servant,

R. Hill

Letter to a Young Man Regarding the Ministry

My Dear Young Friend,

As the office of a minister seems to be beyond all others, I am not surprised that those who feel themselves devoted to God desire to fill that office; and though the groundwork in those who may be called to fill that important trust must be found in a real work of grace upon their own hearts, yet there are other qualifications absolutely needed before they can prove themselves to be workmen who do not need to be ashamed (2 Timothy 2:15). There must be a natural measure of gifts, as well as spiritual graces; and though we may know how far we possess the one by a close examination of our hearts before God, the other, I suppose, can only be discovered to us by a due and proper use of means. There is what the Scripture calls an aptitude to teach (2 Timothy 2:24). This is a quickness and readiness of thought that is well regulated by the letter of the Word and by that *wisdom that is from above* (James 3:17). For the lack of this, many have entered into the ministry and have proven to be a burden to themselves and a dead weight to the churches they may be called to serve.

In my opinion, this holy aptitude can only be learned by the practical exercise of such gifts, and of which others are always better judges than we can be of ourselves. Then such men will be naturally called forth for the further exercise of these gifts by those who have felt the spiritual good of them to their hearts. Then, if Providence sets before you such open doors as these, you can better judge how far you are called to the sacred office. As for all human learning, however good in its place, yet in itself it is nothing; it is much worse than nothing. How many of our half-dead churches are content to be filled with mere pulpit lumber of this sort, while the prosperity even of living churches is greatly hindered by this! In addition to this, jealousy and resentment arise, which too often results in painful divisions and separations, to the disgrace of the sacred cause.

In these few remarks, while I cannot entertain the most distant doubt respecting your lack of integrity and uprightness before God, yet I have lived too long in the world not to know the need of such hints as these, and I am sure you will take them as they are really meant.

Let me also drop a further hint as it respects your present situation in life. All tradesmen who, by their own honesty and integrity, can preserve for themselves an honorable independence, fill a noble situation in life and are not prohibited from being occasionally useful in the church of Christ. At present, you are most usefully engaged in our Sunday schools, and the voluntary services of yourself and others are highly admirable and beneficial to the cause. While thus engaged, you may by degrees feel your way how far the Lord may prepare you for more extended usefulness in the work – and this alone a future day can decide.

And now for my last hint until I will (God willing) again see you in town. A person who enters the ministry, and is compelled to be entirely dependent upon the people for his support, unless he is of remarkable abilities, is frequently called to suffer severely from those who furnish him with his support; and if you would bring up a practical concern, you may suffer for it in a future day. While I would at all times want to live dependent on God, yet it is a great privilege to live a little independent of the world. I will be thankful for both your affliction and for your recovery if it has proved a profitable season for your soul. Sanctified afflictions are spiritual promotions. What a mercy to be improved because of the rod!

With heartfelt love to your family, and all friends, believe me to be,

Very sincerely yours,

Rowland Hill

It is as a preacher of the gospel, after all, that Rowland Hill achieved the greatest and most enduring fame. Preaching was his master passion, and he was still able to exercise his ministry until he was almost eighty-nine years old. When he became too feeble to stand, he would sit on a high stool in the pulpit and talk sweetly upon the text, which was copied in large letters.

He was justly venerated for his character and for his work's sake. His closing years were perhaps his best. The heat of controversy had cooled, and a brighter era had dawned. His heart was at rest in the goodness and mercy of God, and his mind was tranquilized by the divine peace. The wish he had often expressed was fulfilled – that he might die and go home when his work was done. Not long before his last illness, meeting an acquaintance who was nearly as old as himself, he said, "If you and I don't march off soon, our friends up yonder will think we have missed our way."

The testimony of his own conscience to the purity of his motives, and the approving smile of the Savior he had loved so long and had served so well, were conducive to a restfulness of spirit, even in the prospect of a quickly approaching death. "It is a great mercy," he said, "to have a soft pillow under our head in a dying hour; but to enjoy this privilege, remember that we must live near to God."

While he rejoiced in what, through grace, he had been able to accomplish, he, like all true men, had to regret that he had not done more. "Though I don't lament over what I have preached," he wrote to his friend, Mr. W. D. Wills, "yet I greatly lament that I have not preached the same truths with more spirituality, fervor, and devotedness of heart. Though I cannot accuse myself of having been a lazy drone, yet, as a busy bee, oh, that I had been better taught how to collect the sacred honey from those hills from where all our hopes of salvation come!"

Mr. George Clayton described the scene that followed after Rowland Hill had preached for him in York Street Chapel, Walworth, about twelve months before Hill's death:

He retired to the vestry under feelings of great and obvious exhaustion. He remained there until every individual except the ushers, his attendant, and myself had left the place. Eventually and with some reluctance, he seemed to have summoned enough energy to take his departure. Charles, his servant and constant attendant, went before him to open the carriage door. The ushers remained in the vestry. I offered my arm, which he declined, and then I followed him as he passed down the aisle of the chapel. The lights were nearly extinguished, and the silence was profound. Indeed, nothing was heard except the slow, majestic tread of his own footsteps, when in a quiet voice he recited:

And when I'm to die,
   "Receive me," I'll cry,
For Jesus hath loved me,
   I cannot tell why.

But this I can find:
   We two are so joined
He'll not be in glory
   And leave me behind.[10]

To my heart, this was a scene of unequalled solemnity, nor can I ever remember it without a revival of that hallowed, sacred, shuddering sympathy that it originally awakened.

The last address Mr. Hill delivered was to the Sunday school teachers at Surrey Chapel on April 2, 1833. His concluding words were, "*Therefore, my beloved brethren, be ye steadfast*: don't be wavering in any part of your duty; *immovable*: that will prove that you are steadfast indeed, if there is no moving you from it; *always abounding in the work of the Lord* (1 Corinthians 15:58). Remember that it is in time alone that you can do good."

His last illness was very brief, and his consciousness was preserved almost to the end. He said to a visitor at his bedside, "I have no rapturous joys, but peace – a good hope through grace – all through grace." This was a simple but blessed testimony, and as he had lived, so he died, trusting in the infinite merits of his Lord and Savior Jesus Christ. The grace by which he had been sustained *in labors more abundant* (2 Corinthians 11:23) was crowned with glory, and the peace that kept his heart and mind through the last dark valley melted into the fuller peace of heaven's eternal calm!

He died on Thursday evening, April 11, 1833, at the age of eighty-nine. On the Friday of the following week, his mortal

---

10   These stanzas are from a hymn that begins with "O tell me no more," written by John Gambold (1711-1771).

remains were laid to rest in front of the pulpit from which he had dispensed the Word of Life for fifty years.

The large chapel was densely crowded by those who mourned his loss as a father in Israel, a faithful pastor, and a loving and generous friend. The service was conducted by Dr. Rippon, Dr. Collyer, and Thomas Jackson. The funeral sermon was preached by William Jay of Bath, from the text, *Howl, fir tree, for the cedar is fallen* (Zechariah 11:2). And so ended the earthly pilgrimage and the spiritual warfare of one whose unimpeachable character, allegiance to truth, devotion to his calling, and success in the sacred art of soul-winning made him a name to be held in loving remembrance by the entire brotherhood of the redeemed.

A tablet above a sculpture of Rowland Hill was hung on the front of the gallery behind the pulpit, with the following inscription:

TO THE MEMORY OF THE LATE
ROWLAND HILL, A.M.,
FORMERLY OF
SAINT JOHN'S COLLEGE, CAMBRIDGE,

AND FOR

HALF A CENTURY THE ZEALOUS, ACTIVE, AND
DEVOTED
MINISTER OF SURREY CHAPEL,
THIS TABLET IS ERECTED, RATHER IN TOKEN

OF

THE GRATEFUL RECOLLECTIONS OF
A REVERED PASTOR
BY HIS BEREAVED AND MOURNING
CONGREGATION,
THAN AS A TRIBUTE
SUITABLE TO THE WORTH OF ONE,

THE

IMPERISHABLE MONUMENTS OF WHOSE LABORS
ARE THE
NAMES WRITTEN IN HEAVEN OF THE MULTITUDES
LED TO GOD
BY HIS LONG AND FAITHFUL MINISTRY.
HIS MORTAL REMAINS
WERE INTERRED IN THIS CHAPEL ON THE
NINETEENTH DAY OF APRIL,
A.D. MDCCCXXXIII.
BORN 23RD AUGUST, 1744. DIED 11TH APRIL, 1833.

The work that Rowland Hill originated at Surrey Chapel, and maintained with so much vigor, was carried on by his esteemed successor, James Sherman, who was followed by the present pastor, Newman Hall.

Many will regret that the time-honored name of Surrey Chapel has given place to that of Christ Church. The glory of the latter house doubtless exceeds the glory of the former, but the same old gospel will be preached in its integrity, and the philanthropic agencies that have been sustained for nearly one hundred years will renew their youth and be adapted to the spirit and need of the present day.

Chapter 5

Testimonies to His Character and Usefulness

In bringing this brief and imperfect sketch to a close, we add the following testimonies to the character and usefulness of Rowland Hill, written by his contemporaries.

The *Cabinet Annual Register* for 1833 contains the following notice:

Few ministers of the gospel have had to bear the scornful brunt of opposition – to contend against religious animosity, and to bear on through good report, and evil report, through so long and active a career as Mr. Hill. Few have challenged the encounter so boldly, or sustained it so single-handed. The independent and ambiguous ecclesiastical position that he assumed, as theoretically a Churchman, and practically a Dissenter, a Dissenter within the Church, a Churchman among Dissenters – necessarily involved him, especially in the earlier part of his career, in continual polemic skirmishing. His very desire for unity sometimes put on an aggressive form, for of nothing was he so intolerant as of sectarianism. But while he thus made himself many opponents, his blameless character precluded his having any personal enemies. The sarcastic or censorious polemic was forgotten in the warm-hearted philanthropist, the indefatigable evangelist, and the consistent saint. It is quite true that Mr. Hill both occasionally said and did things that few other men could have said with good effect, or done without imprudence. But the unimpeachable integrity and purity of his intentions, the sanctity of his life, the charm of his manners, and the dignity of true breeding, which rescued from coarseness his most familiar phrases and his most eccentric actions, conspired to secure for him, throughout his life, the affectionate veneration of all who enjoyed the privilege of his acquaintance, or understood his character.

In Mr. Hill, an above-average degree of natural shrewdness was combined with an unsuspecting and guileless mind. This sometimes laid him open to presumption. As deep and accurate as his acquaintance with human nature was, he was not always quick-sighted in reading its appearances in the individual. He understood the heart better than the moral appearance of character, and thus his shrewdness did not entirely preserve him from forming mistaken estimates.

His generous benevolence was a distinguishing trait of his character, and he seemed to have the power of inspiring his flock with a similar spirit. On two occasions on which collections were made in the churches and chapels throughout the kingdom (the Patriotic Fund at Lloyd's and the subscription for the relief of the German sufferers), the collections at Surrey Chapel are recorded to have been the largest raised at any one place. The sum annually raised for charitable and religious institutions at the Surrey Chapel has been from £1,500 to £2,000.

As a preacher, Mr. Hill was extremely unequal, as well as systematically unmethodical. He was generally rambling, but to the point, often throwing out the most striking remarks, and sometimes interspersing touches of genuine emotion amid much that bordered upon the ludicrous. But even in his most outlandish quips, there was a redeeming simplicity of purpose and seriousness of intention. You felt that the preacher did not mean to trifle, that there was no attempt at display, no unhallowed familiarity in his feelings or lack of reverence to sacred things. In his more private expository exercises, he was generally serious and edifying, with few irregularities, and often highly impactful. In the devotional part of the service, he was uniformly proper, solemn, and fervent.

Of late years, the majesty of venerable age that invested his appearance added not a little to the impressive effect of his instructions. We will never forget his rising to rebuke the tempestuous discord of the Bible Society Anniversary, held in Exeter Hall, in May 1831. The sharp yet mild reproof came from his lips with almost the force of prophetic authority, and the strong good sense of the few sentences he uttered went directly home to the minds of the audience. His physical powers had long been in a declining state, but his intellectual energies remained almost unimpaired to the end of his existence.

The late Rev. Thomas Jackson, of Stockwell, in the memoir of Mr. Hill furnished to the *Evangelical Magazine,* states:

Perhaps no man in modern times has been more honored than Mr. Hill as the instrument of converting souls. His talent appeared more notably in awakening the careless, instances of which I have had many opportunities of witnessing. I do not remember ever having stayed two days with Mr. Hill in any town without meeting with one or more people to whom his ministry had been made useful.

One case, among many, I cannot omit. The scene occurred at Devonport, Devonshire, after Mr. Hill had been preaching a missionary sermon to a crowded congregation in the large chapel in Prince's Street. The people had withdrawn, and the deacons and a few friends had retired with Mr. Hill into the vestry, when two tall, venerable-looking men, upward of seventy years of age, appeared at the vestry door. After a short pause, they entered, arm in arm, and advanced toward Mr. Hill. With some degree of trepidation, one of them said, "Sir, will you permit two old sinners to have the honor of shaking your hand?"

He replied with some reserve, "Yes, sir," when one of these gentlemen, the other hanging on his arm, took his hand, kissed it, bathed it with his tears, and said, "Sir, do you remember preaching on the spot where this chapel now stands fifty years ago?"

"Yes, I do," was the reply. The old man then proceeded to say, "Oh, sir! I can never forget the dear friend who has hold of my arm, nor can I ever forget that sermon. We were then two careless young men, in His Majesty's dockyard, rushing to destruction as fast as time and sin could take us there. Having heard that an interesting young clergyman was to preach out of doors, we determined to go and have some fun. Accordingly, we loaded our pockets with stones, intending to pelt you; but, sir, when you arrived, our courage failed, and as soon as you engaged in prayer, we were so deeply impressed that we looked at each other and trembled. When you named your text and began to speak, the word came with power to our hearts. The big tears rolled down our cheeks. We put our hands into our pockets and dropped the stones one after another until they were all gone, for God had taken the stones out of our hearts. When the service was over, we left, but our hearts were too full to speak until we came near to our lodgings, when my friend at my elbow said, 'John, this will not do. We are both wrong; good night.'

"This was all he could utter. He went to his apartment, and I to mine, but neither of us dared to go to bed lest we should awake in hell. From that time, sir, we humbly hope we were converted to God, who, of His infinite mercy, has kept us in His ways to the present moment; and we thought, sir, if you would permit us, after the lapse of half a hundred years, to have the pleasure of shaking your hand before we go home, it would be the greatest honor that could be given to us."

Mr. Hill was deeply affected. The tears rolled down his venerable cheeks in quick succession. He fell on the necks of the old men quite in the patriarchal style, and then you could have seen them, locked in each other's arms, weeping tears of holy joy and gratitude to the Father of mercies. It was a scene at which Gabriel might have rejoiced, and faithlessness might have turned pale. I am aware that I cannot do justice to it by my description, although I feel, at this distance of time, something like celestial pleasure in recording what I then witnessed.

In a sermon preached on Sunday, March 3, 1833, at the chapel in Blackfriars Road, London, Mr. Hill gave an interesting narrative in the following words: "I am an old man, and I am exhorting you with my remaining strength not to be conformed to this world, but to be followers of Him who, when your flesh and your heart fail you, will be the strength of your heart and your portion forever (Psalm 73:26). There are many of you now hearing me who have not made up your minds on this subject. Oh, if I were a young man, how I would work you! There is a great difference in the manner and method of worshipping God, adopted by different Christians, and for my own part I am not particular. I do not care how a man worships God as long as he worships Him in spirit and in truth. I do not mind going a little out of the regular road with a man if it falls in with his inclination, and in this way I would become all things to all men, with the hope, through grace, of winning souls to Christ (1 Corinthians 9:22). A man may lead me along with him very easily, as long as he does not lead me into sin, but the moment he attempts to do this, we part company. Let me call especially on the young around me not to be conformed to this world, for we cannot walk two ways at the same time: *Ye cannot serve God and mammon* (Matthew 6:24).

"It has been many years since a young man, who had been conformed to this world and who had lived a very wicked life, made up his mind to come to this chapel to hear the man preach who, in his estimation, was beside himself. He came, and He who by the foolishness of preaching can make many wise (1 Corinthians 1:21), put words into my mouth to suit his case. He went away sorrowing, with an arrow in his heart. He had a brother who had pursued the same thoughtless, ungodly course as himself, and he told him where he had been and how he felt. 'Brother,' he said, 'we have lived very wicked lives. I wish you would come with me, for I think if you were to hear the same man preach, you would feel the same as I do.' His brother consented, and they both came here and sat, as you are now sitting, to hear the Word of God preached by His unworthy servant. I had this account from the young man who first came, and he told me that if ever he had enjoyed a happy moment in the course of his life, it was when, turning around to his brother, he saw the repentant tear trickling down his cheek. These two young men became servants of God, and although one of them is dead, yet they are servants of God still. The one worships God at His throne, and the other at His footstool."

Personal Reminiscences by an Old Member of Surrey Chapel

The first time I had the honor of being in Mr. Hill's company was at a committee meeting of the Southwark Sunday School Society, of which he was president. He was then considerably advanced in years, and the strong man had begun to bow. His step was slow and frail, but his body was erect. His grey hair was brushed back from his forehead, exhibiting a noble countenance so gentle and kind that all the compassionate feelings of the heart were instantly attracted toward him. We all rose to receive him as he entered, which he courteously acknowledged by a pleasant smile and the witty exclamation, "Here's a resurrection!" His inquiries into the state and discipline of the schools were searching and detailed, and his remarks full of wisdom, though at the same time full of that quiet humor that made his conversation not only profitable, but amusing. He contrasted the then present times with those when Sunday schools did not exist, and he expressed his earnest hope that before long the religious instruction of children would form part of the operation of every Christian church. "We should get at them," he said, "as soon as we can. The devil begins early enough; if possible, let us get the advantage over him by getting to work before he does."

Reference having been made to his early itinerant labors, he remarked, "God was pleased to smile upon these poor efforts, but I could not do now as I did then. Time has taken me by the hand. I have known what it is to preach twenty-one sermons for twenty-one meals."

During the evening, an inquiry was made concerning a teacher who had been under considerable obligations to Mr. Hill, and had once rendered us good service, but whose zeal had considerably abated. Rowland Hill then said, "Steadfast and unmovable, *always abounding in the work of the Lord* (1 Corinthians 15:58); let that be our motto. I thought that man would have continued to be a great assistance to us, but I am disappointed." And then with a characteristically amusing expression of countenance, he added, "If anyone has got him at the bottom of his pocket, I wish he would pull him out."

Toward the close of the business, Mr. Hill announced the receipt of a donation from a nobleman, who at his solicitation had attended an annual meeting of the teachers. "I am glad," said the treasurer, "that he has become acquainted with our operations, for I believe he is a good man, and a man of great influence."

"Well," replied the president, with one of his comical looks, "I think he is more enlightened upon the subject now than he was, for I have explained to him not only the manner in which you operate, but also the way you are, in your turn, sometimes operated upon. At the meeting he said to me, 'Are these your teachers?' 'Yes,' I answered, 'I believe so, with, perhaps, a few exceptions.' 'I suppose,' he remarked again, 'they make a pretty good thing of it. They seem respectably dressed.' 'I expect,' I said, 'they are pretty well satisfied. I hear no complaints.' 'If it is a fair question,' continued his lordship, 'what do they receive for their services?' 'As to that,' I replied, 'it is very little of this world's goods that they get, unless it is now and then a flea, or another insect not quite so nimble in its movements.'"

If anyone had been present that evening who had imbibed the notion that religion makes people sad, I think the error would have been laughed out of him.

Although Mr. Hill was a great wit and was exceedingly amusing in conversation, he was a very different man in the pulpit. There he seemed conscious of standing on holy ground, and his words were solemn, weighty, and impressive. It is true that he sometimes used expressions that created a smile. With a mind constituted as his was, how could it be otherwise? As to those crude and absurd utterances that many were so fond of putting into his mouth, they rest upon no foundation of truth whatsoever. It was his complaint, and it was the heaviest charge I ever heard him bring against his countrymen, that people would not allow him to be a gentleman. I had the privilege of sitting under his ministry for more than twelve years, and I can truthfully affirm that I never heard him utter a sentence unbecoming an ambassador of Christ or the sanctity of the pulpit. Still, I am not certain whether these foolish reports did not, in the end, do more good than real mischief.

One Sunday morning, as I was about to proceed to my accustomed place of worship, a female friend waited upon me in the company of two farming men who lived a good distance away. She told me they had a great desire to hear Mr. Hill, and she asked me to take them with me and get them seated in a favorable position. I willingly undertook the commission. As we proceeded on our way, the two men asked me many questions about "Sir Rowland," as they called him, and informed me of many things they had heard about him. "They tell me," one of the men said, "that he says that religion is like a round of beef, if it is cut and come again."

"Well," I replied, "he often makes use of very homely expressions, but I do not remember ever having heard him make that remark." Strangely enough, that very morning we were favored with something close to it. I took the men into my pew, and for some time they seemed to take the greatest interest in everything that was going on; but when the venerable preacher ascended to the pulpit, every other object ceased to attract their attention. "There he is," said one to the other, "there he is." "Yes," replied his companion. "How happy he looks."

His subject was "the gospel of our salvation," and as he proceeded with his discourse, my two friends began to be evidently excited. The fullness and freeness of that salvation, a topic always delightful to his soul, was set forth in burning words, and their excitement increased. "It is free," he exclaimed, "free as the air you breathe. And it is as full as it is free. There is enough for all. I never heard a man say to his neighbor, 'Don't you breathe so much air; if you do, there will not be enough for me to breathe.' No, there is sufficient for everyone, and all are invited to come to the gospel feast. 'In My Father's house is bread enough and to spare.' It is 'cut and come again.'"

At this, the delighted countrymen rose to their feet and stretched themselves forward as if unable any longer to control their feelings. I became alarmed lest their emotions would find vent in some audible exclamation, so I gently touched the one next to me, and smilingly motioned him to resume his seat. To my great relief, he immediately complied. The other man followed his example after he had given a few violent nods of satisfaction, and I was enabled once more to breathe freely.

* * * * *

I have sometimes listened to conversations between Mr. Hill and one or two of his friends in which the remarkable energy that characterized his more youthful ministry was referred to. From these discourses, it appeared that he had been accustomed to stamp violently with his foot, thump his Bible, and even stretch himself over his desk and strike the front of the pulpit. On one occasion, a friend who had traveled with him in Scotland said to him, "I will never forget that sermon you preached in the old church at K—. It was an excellent discourse."

"Yes," replied the veteran, with a kind of frown, "I remember the devil told me that before I left the pulpit."

"At any rate," said the friend, "it was followed by the divine blessing. There was a great awakening among the people. That is the main thing."

He replied, "It is a poor sermon, no matter how noisy or eloquent, that merely tickles the ear without touching the heart."

The friend continued, "You thundered away at a fine rate that morning. I will venture to say that the pulpit cushion had not received such a punishment for many years, for it was a very lifeless minister who regularly preached there. In a few minutes, you raised such a cloud of dust as nearly hid you from my view. Some, who did not gain admittance, told me they heard you very well in the churchyard."

"Ah," replied Mr. Hill thoughtfully, "things have changed since then. The bulldog has got old and cannot bark quite as loud. It is a great mercy that he can bark at all."

* * * * *

At Easter, Mr. Hill was accustomed to invite the children of the neighboring schools to assemble in Surrey Chapel to receive an address – the boys on Monday and the girls on Tuesday. Strangers were not expected to be present. Still, many would generally make their way in with the children, for the doors were not strictly guarded, and females, who were ignorant of the regulations, would frequently appear among the boys. On these occasions, nothing seemed to disturb his composure more than to discover a bonnet among the bare heads of the boys, and he would never rest until it had disappeared.

Upon coming one day to the front of the pulpit for the purpose of making his usual inspection, he was annoyed by the appearance of a whole row of females who were sitting near the front entrance. Having sent a messenger to them in vain, he determined to take the matter into his own hands. In a voice that produced an immediate silence among the children, he exclaimed, "I fear there is some mistake. Yes, it must be so," he continued, shading his face from the light with his hand, as if to make himself quite certain of the fact. "If I am not greatly in error, there are some young men who have come into the chapel with women's bonnets on." All eyes were instantly turned toward the place to which his eyes were directed, and a shout of laughter was raised by the whole youthful congregation (numbering at that time about two thousand) that continued until the fair intruders, not being able to stand against such artillery, one by one lowered their colors and left.

* * * * *

Dr. Stoughton says, "You must think of his appearance: a fine, noble, expressive countenance; eloquent eyes; an imperial nose; an erect gait; tall and commanding: the perfect gentleman." Stoughton also judges Hill's character as an element of success:

Rowland Hill was an extraordinary man, and in estimating a man's life, you must look at him as a whole. I believe that in the effect produced by eminent persons, what they are goes far more than what they simply do. When you analyze a minister's acts, sermons, speeches, and so on, you are sometimes surprised. You might ask, "How do you account for the results? How is it that he exerts such an influence? I do not see anything so very wonderful in what he says!" Perhaps not, but take him altogether! The sum total of his nature, character, and habits will throw light on the question. No doubt, many who heard Rowland Hill thought they could preach better, and taking some single sermon as an example, they probably could – but their life altogether was a different thing from his!

> I would express him simple, grave, sincere;
> In doctrine uncorrupt; in language plain,
> And plain in manner; decent, solemn, chaste,
> And natural in gesture; much impressed
> Himself, as conscious of his awful charge,
> And anxious mainly that the flock he feeds
> May feel it too; affectionate in look,
> And tender in address, as well becomes
> A messenger of grace to guilty men.[11]

---

11   This is from *The Task* by William Cowper (1731-1800).

Part 2

Anecdotes

Chapter 6

Anecdotes

A Just Rebuke

An Antinomian who was addicted to drinking rudely asked him, "Do you think, Mr. Hill, that a glass of alcohol would drive grace out of my heart?"

"No," he answered, "for there is none in it."

A False Professor

A lady who professed the religion of the Savior, but whose daily practice was not in harmony with it, once said to him, "Oh! I am afraid lest, after all, I should not be saved."

"I am glad to hear you say so," replied Mr. Hill, "for I have been long afraid for you, I assure you."

A Lady's Temper

"I once had tea with a lady," he said, "who was very particular about her china. The servant unfortunately broke the best bread-and-butter plate. Her mistress took very little notice of the circumstance at the time, only remarking, 'Never mind, Mary – never mind; accidents cannot be prevented.'

"'She will let me have it some time soon,' said the servant, after she left the room; and so it turned out. The good woman's temper was corked up for a season, but it came out with terrible vengeance after the company left."

Freedom in Service

Mr. Hill always spoke of his Master's "sweet service" as being "perfect freedom." In one week, when past the age of seventy-one, he traveled a hundred miles in a mountainous part of Wales and preached twenty-one sermons! Sometimes he complained that he was tired on a Sunday evening, but the energy of his conversation and the liveliness of his manner used occasionally to elicit the remark, "Well, sir, yours is a curious sort of fatigue." To this, he would reply, "I was tired just now, but I forgot it."

Efforts for Children

When Mr. Hill was prevented from reading by attacks of inflammation in the eyes, to which he was subject, he found a source of amusement in making little boxes covered with colored paper, containing in partitions the letters of the alphabet, as presents for the children of his friends. In each box there were printed directions that showed how sentences and texts of Scripture could be found, with a couplet in rhyme on every letter. Mr. Hill could often be seen hard at work, cutting out the letters that he had had printed on pasteboard for the purpose, with the greatest apparent earnestness. While at Bristol in 1824, he sent a sample of his invention to Christian author Mrs. Hannah More, and in the letter that accompanied it, he humorously imitated the style of Sternhold and Hopkins, who had put the entire book of Psalms in rhyme so it could be sung in churches:

With this my love doth come to you:
My love it is both sure and true,
And eke the same, likewise also,
Unto your household it doth go.

Diversion, Shoemaking

Mr. Hill also made beautiful little shoes for infants, and would sometimes promise to his female friends, on their marriage, that he would present the firstborn with a pair of nursery slippers. He had a pattern of the various parts, from which he cut out the shoe and then sewed them together with very great neatness. These little productions of a great man were much valued by those who were fortunate enough to receive them.

Diversion, Gardening

His garden was a source of perpetual enjoyment to him, and his gardens were wonderful. The strawberries, melons, and fruit trees were brought to near perfection under his own special care.

After dinner, while some person read aloud, he was busily occupied in making nets for his fruit trees or fishponds, and if he took a walk in the evening, he would sometimes measure the distance from the house at Wotton to some place in the vicinity.

Concern for Man and Animals

When Mr. Hill was traveling, he felt much interest for the comfortable accommodation of his attendant. At a friend's house in Kent, where he was to sleep, he said to his host, "I suppose my helper had better get a bed at the inn."

"No, sir," was the reply, "we have provided for him." Mr. Hill was evidently pleased.

Mr. Hill was also merciful to his animals. His horses were his constant care. Even his domestic cat and other creatures shared largely in his daily concern.

Cleanliness Next to Godliness

Mr. Hill frequently visited some of the gloomy shacks that abound in the neighborhood of Surrey Chapel, several of which were inhabited by pious poor. He spoke to them in tender sympathy and the most lovely humility. He always strongly urged upon the poor the necessity of every possible adornment of the Christian character, especially cleanliness.

The least symptom of untidiness was noticed by him in an instant with, "Here, mistress, is a little money for you to buy some soap and a scrub brush; there is plenty of water to be had for nothing."

The Power of a Holy Character

In one of his visits of mercy to Gloucester jail, Rowland Hill met with a man to whom his conversation appeared to be useful. Hill exercised his influence on the prisoner's behalf, and succeeded not only in saving his life, but eventually in obtaining his freedom. Once the man left the prison, he could not find any employment due to lack of a good character, so Mr. Hill compassionately took him into his employ as a gardener. The man conducted himself with much decency for a considerable time.

Such, however, was the deceitfulness of the heart that the man afterward resumed his former wicked pursuits, was tried for several robberies, was condemned to death, and was eventually executed. His benevolent master again visited him in his cell, and during the conversations he had with him, the prisoner confessed that he had made frequent attempts to break into Mr. Hill's house after he left his service. He said that he had hidden himself several times near the premises, but had always been prevented from accomplishing his purpose by the remembrance of his master's great kindness to him and a fearful and overwhelming impression that God was in the place.

Visits to Criminals

During his visits with criminals condemned to death, Mr. Hill preserved so much composure that none but those who knew him well were aware of the depth of feeling concealed beneath his calm exterior. After his return from these painful visits, his dinner was generally sent away scarcely tasted, and he gave vent to his previously suppressed emotions by frequent comments, whispering with solemnity, as if unconscious of the presence of another: "Condemned to die! Condemned to die! God, what a mercy to be kept from sin by the restraining grace of Your Holy Spirit!"

The Secret of a Long Life

In reference to some things that had been said upon his good old age, he remarked, "I daresay you young ministers would be glad to live to be old men. Now I will tell you how to attain your wishes: preach three times a day, and seven days in the week, and then you will find not only that you are in a fine state of health, but that you stand a good chance of becoming old men. A good pulpit perspiration is a well-known thing to keep a man in good health."

Socinianism Attacked

In one of his journeys in 1825, Mr. Hill attacked the errors of Socinians in no very gentle terms. Some people who observed this said rather sneeringly, "Poor old gentleman! It is a pity he does not stop." This came to his ears, and after a very animated address on a public occasion, he suddenly said, in his own incomparable manner, after explaining the cause of the remark, "The poor old gentleman will never stop until the power to refute errors and spread the truth leaves him. Any further kind advice on this subject will only be thrown away."

A Disreputable Preacher Rebuked

Mr. Hill sometimes rendered a word of rebuke equally strong and witty. Thus, when a preacher of no very good reputation was in the vestry of a place where he was going to preach, and seemed uneasy that his attendant would not arrive in time with his gown, Mr. Hill said, "Sir, you need not be uneasy, for I can preach without my gown, but I cannot preach without my character."

A Parenthesis

Mr. Jay said, "When Mr. Hill was preaching for me once, I remember what an impression he made by the use of an interjective parenthesis. When reading 1 Thessalonians 5, he repeated the verse, *Abstain from all appearance of evil*. He then lifted his eyes and said in a solemn voice, 'Oh, the infinite delicacy of the gospel!'"

A Pointed Comment

In the pulpit one day, he read the words of the woman of Samaria at the well: *The Jews have no dealings with the Samaritans* (John 4:9). Looking off as if he saw the parties themselves, he exclaimed, "But the devil has had dealings enough with you both."

A Faithful Reproof

Mr. Hill was sometimes very delightfully appropriate in his manner of giving reproof, and it was done in a way unique to himself. He was once present when arrangements were being made for the organization of a public society, and the people present were talking over the names of the individuals who should be proposed to a general meeting as appropriate members of the committee. Several names of tradesmen having been mentioned, a gentleman offered his advice by remarking that he thought some regard should be paid to the respectability of the society, and that "tag, rag, and bobtail should not compose the committee." Mr. Hill easily saw through the flimsy charade that poorly concealed the pride of the human heart. Therefore, he stood up, lifted up his hands as in the attitude of prayer, and exclaimed, "God bless tag, God bless rag, and God bless bobtail!" Having uttered these words, he sat down, and the tradesmen were placed on the committee without another word in the way of opposition.

Mr. Hill and the Boxer

Mr. Hill was once scheduled to preach in a town where he expected to be violently opposed, and where it was known that a famous boxer was committed to harass him. Nevertheless, he was determined to preach, and therefore came up with a plan by which to disarm his opponent of his fierceness.

Having ascended the pulpit, and satisfying himself from the appearance of the boxer that he was not inaccessible to flattery, Hill motioned for him to come to the pulpit stairs. He told the boxer that he had come to preach to these people in the hope of doing them good, but that some opposition had been threatened. Rowland Hill said that he had been told of the man's strength and skill in self-defense and had full confidence in his powers. Therefore, Hill said that he would place himself in his hands, rely on his protection, and asked for the honor of his company to ride with him in his carriage after the service to dinner!

The man felt the full force of the compliment, and all his animosity was removed. He declared his readiness to defend the preacher in the case of any insult being offered, and he was as good as his word. He accompanied Mr. Hill to dinner, and ever after boasted of the honor that Mr. Hill had bestowed upon him.

Laodicean Christians

W. Jay writes: "His brother, Sir Richard, once told me of an early instance of his cleverness, remarking that he was the same as a boy. It occurred while he was at Eton College. Even then, he was under deep impressions of a religious nature, and as he felt the importance of divine things himself, he was active and concerned to do good to others. This is what he did in regard to an old female servant who frequently waited upon him. One day she quite reproved him for his zeal, saying that people should not be excessively righteous and should be careful to avoid extremes in religion. 'Some,' she said, 'were too cold, and some were too hot.' 'Then,' said young Rowland, 'I suppose you think we had better be lukewarm?' 'Yes,' she said, 'that was the proper middle ground.' He then took up his New Testament and read the Savior's address to the church of Laodicea: *I would thou wert cold or hot. So then because thou art lukewarm, and neither cold nor hot, I will spue thee out of my mouth* (Revelation 3:15-16). At hearing this, his halfhearted admonisher seemed a little surprised and stood astounded."

Mr. Hill's Story of a Preaching Farmer

A certain farmer, well-known to me, was always moral, yet ignorant of the gospel. By reading some of the sermons of the late Mr. William Romaine, he was called to the knowledge of the truth. The farmer was a man of good sense and great integrity, and he now understood that his workers should not live without family worship. The Bible was almost as much in sight in his kitchen as the bacon rack, and when he read the Bible to them, he could not refrain from expressing the simple feelings of his heart. He wept, and they wept in unison. In prayer, he found he was not lacking in *the spirit of grace and of supplications* (Zechariah 12:10). Thus being enabled to tell his own needs before his family, they began to find out their needs also. This answered the purpose. The family was filled with surprise, and they surprised their neighbors, who quietly entered their home to join in their worship.

They now requested him to preach, but the modest farmer resisted the call. He had a gracious sister who told him not to fight against God, for others besides his own family benefited by their attendance. The farmer consented, yet he was no enthusiast, but a solid, pious, thinking man, and had a good knowledge of the Bible. No man of good sense, even though he has never studied Greek, Latin, or logic, will ever talk nonsense. Thus he began as a preacher, and he was wonderfully blessed. He became quite the apostle, the reformer of the neighborhood. The generous public soon accommodated the farmer with a convenient place of worship in the town. The farmer was solemnly ordained to the pastoral charge, and the communion among them was very seriously and largely attended.

Husbands, Love Your Wives

Mr. Hill often felt very troubled at the false reports that were circulated about many of his sayings, especially those regarding his publicly mentioning Mrs. Hill. His attentions to her until the end of life were of the most gentlemanly and affectionate kind. The high view he held of her may be seen from the following fact. A friend once informed Mr. Hill of the sudden death of a lady, the wife of a minister, and remarked, "I am afraid our dear minister loved his wife too well, and the Lord, in wisdom, has removed her."

"What, sir?" replied Mr. Hill with the deepest feeling. "Can a man love a good wife too much? Impossible, sir, unless he can love her better than Christ loves the church: *Husbands, love your wives, even as Christ also loved the church, and gave Himself for it*" (Ephesians 5:25).

Dissension Rebuked

It once happened at his own house that two people of opposite views regarding church government grew heated in their argument and appealed to him. He said, "Well, I must say you are both wrong. I was just thinking that if you were tied together by the tail, like two cats, and thrown over a forked stick, you would scratch each other's eyes out."

Wapping Sinners

When preaching at St. John's Church in Wapping on one occasion, and observing that his audience was unusually large and made up mainly of seafaring persons, he remarked, "I am come to preach to great sinners, notorious sinners, profane sinners," and then he exclaimed with special emphasis, "yes, to Wapping sinners."

Justice before Generosity

Once, when preaching for a public charity, a note was handed to him in the pulpit asking if it would be right for someone who was bankrupt to contribute to the collection. He referred to the inquiry, and answered it firmly in the negative. He then added, "But, my friends, I would advise you who are not bankrupt to be sure to contribute to the offering plate this evening, or the people will be sure to say, 'There is the bankrupt person.'"

A Cautious Preacher

Rowland Hill once said of a man who knew the truth, but seemed afraid to preach it in its fullness, "He preaches the truth as a donkey mumbles a thistle – very cautiously."

The Light of the Heathen

Preaching on one occasion in a country village, and wanting simply to answer the question, "Do not the heathen have sufficient light?" his illustration was exceedingly simple and clear. "I admit," he said, "that the heathen have some natural light, but they do not use even this properly. Now suppose the whole family in a farmhouse assembled around the large kitchen fire on a winter's evening, all peaceful and happy. Soon the stableman opens the door and cries out, 'Master! Master! The thieves are robbing the henhouse!' They all jump up. The farmer rushes to his closet for his lantern. He lights the candle and runs out, and holding up the light nearly to his head, advances with cautious steps. The wheelbarrow has been left in the way, and the good man falls over it. Why? Is it because he has no light? No. It is because he used it improperly. It is the same with the heathen."

Plain Preaching Commended

After hearing an elaborate sermon that lacked power, Mr. Hill said, "That cut-and-dried stuff never tells. It does not get hold of the people. It is too fine by half. There was once a man who preached for me at Wotton, and he used such difficult words that the people could not understand him. Some of the plain folks used to say to me, when I came from London, "We know what we hear when you preach, but Mr.— uses so many dictionary words that we can't understand his meaning. We don't know where he gets them unless it is out of the almanac."

On one occasion, he said, "It is astonishing what nonsense some people will talk in the pulpit. When I was out the other day on a missionary journey, I heard of a man who had been preaching on modern improvement, and among other things, of the merciful way of making war since the invention of gunpowder, which proved so much easier a death than that inflicted by the ancient weapons. He got what he deserved for his efforts, for they have called him the gunpowder parson ever since." Then he added, "I preach Christ crucified, and when that ceases to be my only theme, may I cease from the pulpit."

The Penalty of Popularity

Mr. Hill was so well known that requests of all kinds were made to him, and when it was learned that he was in town, people literally knocked on his door from morning until night. Nothing could exceed the good humor with which he submitted to every type of interruption. Foreigners, beggars, candidates for the ministry – almost every person who called found him ready to listen to their cases. These were sometimes not a little strange. One evening, after dinner, his servant said, "Sir, a foreign gentleman would like to speak to you."

"Well, show him in," said Mr. Hill, and then a tall, moustached man entered who addressed him with, "Mister Hill, I have heard you are a wonderful, great, good man. Can you do anything?"

"Mercy on us! I must be a wonderful man."

"Yes, sir, you are a wonderful man, so I call to ask you to make my ambassador do his duty by me."

"Sir, I can assure you I do not have the honor of knowing him."

"Oh, sir, but he would pay attention to a letter from you."

"Sir, I can have no possible influence with him, and cannot take the liberty of writing to him on a subject about which I know nothing."

"But sir, I will tell you."

Finding his visitor to be stubborn, he concluded the business by saying, "Well, sir, you may give my compliments to the ambassador, and say that I advise him to do his duty; that will do as well as writing."

"Very good, sir. Good day."

Rocking-Horse Christians

Entering the house of one of his congregation, he saw a child on a rocking horse. "Dear me," exclaimed the aged minister, "how wondrously like some Christians! There is motion, but no progress." The rocking-horse type of spiritual life is still characteristic of too many church members in the present day. *Grow in grace* (2 Peter 3:18) is an exhortation too little regarded.

The Deserted Lamb

Mr. Hill once said, "Walking through my field on a winter's morning, I came across a lamb that I thought was dead, but lifting it up, I found it just barely alive. The cruel mother had almost starved it to death. I put it into my arms and brought it into my house. There I rubbed its starved limbs, warmed it by the fireside, and fed it with warm milk from the cow. Soon the lamb revived. First it was afraid of me, but afterward it thoroughly loved me. I mostly fed it with my own hand, so it followed me wherever I went, bleating after me whenever it saw me. It was always happy when it could frisk around me, but it was never so pleased as when I would carry it in my arms. Jesus is a Shepherd – the Shepherd of souls – and of Him it is said that He carries the lambs in His bosom, and gently leads those that are with young (Isaiah 40:11). If you desire to love Jesus, read that blessed book, the Bible, for there you hear such things of the love of Christ to poor ruined sinners that I hope will melt your eyes to tears and your hearts into love."

Fire Low

Mr. Hill always wanted to be considered the apostle of the common people, following Him whom the common people heard gladly (Mark 12:37), and in whose teaching the poor had the gospel preached unto them (Matthew 11:5). He who undertakes this work of faith and labor of love will find that he does not have to address angels, or sometimes hardly even people. He will need to learn the advice that the philosopher gave his pupils: "Study the people," or that which Cromwell gave to his soldiers: "Fire low." If his men had fired high, they would have accomplished no more than some of our preachers who shoot over their hearers' heads.

Temptation to Desertion

Howell Harris, one of Mr. Whitefield's most energetic followers, was a man of extraordinary powers of body and mind. Harris used to tell that once when he was on a journey through Wales, he was subjected to great temptations to desert his Master's cause, when he said, "Satan, I'll match you for this!" "And so I did," he added, "for I had not ridden many miles before I came to a place where the people were being amused and entertained. There was a show of charlatans, which I entered, and just as they were beginning, I jumped into the midst of them and cried out, 'Let us pray,' which so stunned them that they listened to me quietly while I preached them a most tremendous sermon that frightened many of them home."

Rowland Hill greatly delighted in this anecdote, and often considered that amid somewhat similar scenes he had been enabled successfully to assail the kingdom of Satan.

Enthusiasm

Once, at Wotton, he was completely carried away by the impassioned rush of his feelings, and raising himself to his full stature, he exclaimed, "Because I am being honest and sincere, people call me an enthusiast, but I am not. Mine are the words of truth and sincerity. When I first came into this part of the country, I was walking on a distant hill, and I saw a gravel pit fall in and bury three human beings alive. I lifted up my voice for help so loud that I was heard in the town below, a mile away. Help came and rescued two of the poor sufferers. No one called me an enthusiast then, and when I see eternal destruction ready to fall upon poor sinners, about to hopelessly bury them in an eternal mass of woe, and I call aloud for them to escape, shall I be called an enthusiast now? No, no!"

A Convenient Umbrella

On a wet day, a number of people took shelter in his chapel during a heavy shower while he was preaching. He remarked,

"Many people are greatly to be blamed for making their religion a cloak, but I do not think they are much better who make it an umbrella."

A Minister's Temper

Mr. Hill used to urge all who entered the sacred office to realize the necessity of maintaining Christian temperament among their people. "Some folks," he would say, "appear as if they had been bathed in vinegar in their infancy, which penetrated through their skins and has made them sour-blooded ever since; but this will not do for a messenger of the gospel. As he bears a message, so he must manifest a spirit of love."

The Barber and the Wig

He was once addressing a number of candidates for the ministry, and he said, "I will tell you a story. A barber had made a good living and retired to his native place, where he became a preacher in a small chapel. Another person from the same village, being similarly fortunate, settled there also, and attended the ministry of the barber-preacher. Wanting a new wig, he said to his pastor, 'You might as well make it for me.' The pastor agreed to do so. However, the wig was sent home badly made, but the pastor charged the man nearly double the usual price! The good man said nothing, but when anything especially profitable escaped the lips of the preacher, he observed to himself, 'Excellent words, but oh, the wig!' When the barber prayed with apparent passion, he also thought, 'This should touch my heart, but oh, the wig!' Now, my dear young brethren, wherever you are placed, remember the to be honest in everything you do, or it will weaken your ministry."

Preaching to Sailors

He once paid a visit to Portsmouth. He had the greatest pleasure in laboring among sailors, and he generally found his way to their hearts and affections. Many sturdy sailors who denounced his opening address with an oath melted into tears before the close of his solemn appeal. Tears often filled the eyes and dropped down the rough cheek of some veteran sailor who, until touched with the story of the Savior's love and sufferings, seemed as hard and sapless as the oak that carried him across the ocean where, without a thought of judgment or eternity, he had sternly risked his life in the service of his country.

Mr. Hill frequently experienced the rough grasp of some sailor's hand who had been brought to a knowledge of the way of life by a sermon he had come to sneer at and oppose. He used to say about his visits to seaports, "I was most affected by those who came up to me and told me in tears that I had led them to Christ the last time I was there; this always touches me." When they abused, pelted, and threatened him, he stood calm and unmoved. His countenance, capable of almost every expression, never assumed that of fear, but as soon as anyone told him, in a way that removed all doubt, that he had been the means of bringing him to God, he could never hold back his emotion.

Caught by Guile

In the early period of his ministry, when visiting one of our seaport towns where he attempted to preach in the open air, he was so interrupted by noise and projectiles that it was impossible for a time to proceed. He was on horseback, and his footman was with him. Instead of attempting to preach, he resorted to an innocent strategy. Addressing the people, he said, "My lads, I have no right over you. If you do not choose to hear me, I have no authority to force your attention, but I have traveled some miles for the sake of doing or receiving good. I have, therefore, a proposal to make. I always did admire British sailors. I see here some able-bodied sailors. Some of you, no doubt, have seen a great deal of service and have been in many storms. Some of you may have been in dangerous shipwrecks. Now, as I am very excited to hear the adventures of sailors, my proposal is that as many of you who desire to, one at a time, stand up and tell us what you have seen and suffered, and what dangers you have escaped. I will sit and listen to all you have to say, upon this condition – that you agree to hear me afterward."

This proposal made many of them laugh enthusiastically, and they said one to another, "Stand up and give us a lecture!" One called upon a talkative sailor by name: "I say, Harry, you give him a lecture!" That produced a loud burst of laughter through the whole crowd. To keep them in a good mood, Mr. Hill laughed with them.

After waiting some time, Mr. Hill asked, "Will none of you take my proposal?" None being disposed to do so, he said, "I am a clergyman. I came, not long ago, from the University of Cambridge. If you would have heard me, I would have told you nothing except what is in the Bible. I will tell you what I intended to say if you had heard me quietly."

Then, beginning with a declaration of the grace and compassion of Christ in dying to save all repentant sinners, he led them to the consideration of the thief on the cross, and then to the character and circumstances of the prodigal son and the compassion of his father. His description of what he would have said was so interesting and affecting that he riveted their attention and produced an evident change in their attitude toward him. While he was speaking, they gradually drew nearer, hanging, as is the practice of sailors when standing in a crowd, upon each other's shoulders. In this position they listened with almost deathlike silence until he had finished telling them what he would have said if they had been willing to hear him. He then took off his hat, bowed to them, and thanked them for their civility. Most of them took off their hats and gave him three cheers. Several men yelled out, "When will you come again, sir?" One man, who seemed to be the champion of the whole group, said, "If you will come again, sir, no one will hurt a hair of your head if I am on shore."

Mighty Fine Preachers

Thomas Jackson said, "Rowland Hill was a strange compound of wisdom, good sense, whimsicalness, and piety." There was no pretense in his style. He was perfectly natural, and he tried to achieve the end in view by the most direct and efficient means. "I don't like those mighty fine preachers," he said, "who so beautifully round off all their sentences that they are sure to roll off the sinner's conscience."

An Inscription for a Clock

A clock having the following original lines inscribed on it was presented to Pomarre, King of Otaheite (Tahiti), by Rowland Hill:

> Master, behold me, here I stand,
> To tell the hours at thy command.
> What is thy will? 'Tis my delight
> To serve thee both by day and night.
> Master, be wise, and learn from me
> To serve thy God as I serve thee.

Salvation to the Uttermost

When Rowland Hill was a young man, he was on a visit to Mr. Whitefield, who asked him to call on a poor woman who had been so dreadfully burned that she could not survive many hours. He went immediately and prayed with her. He had no sooner left her than she called out, "Oh, where is Mr. Whitefield?" Urged by her pleading, her friends requested a second time for Whitefield to visit her. Mr. Hill went and again prayed with her. The poor afflicted woman continued still to desire Whitefield's presence. When her friends came for him a third time, "I begged of him," said Mr. Hill, "not to go, for he could hardly expect to do any good. I told Mr. Whitefield, 'Your nerves are too weak and your feelings are too delicate to endure such scenes.' I will never forget his mild rebuke: 'Permit me; my Master can save to the uttermost, to the very uttermost'" (Hebrews 7:25).

Stinginess Rebuked

In rebuking the stinginess of some people, he said, "There is a perpetual frost in the pockets of some wealthy people; as soon as they put their hands into them, they are frozen, and they are unable to bring out their money. If I had my way, I would hang all misers, but the reverse of the common mode. I would hang them up by the heels so that their money might run out of their pockets for you to pick up and put in the plate."

A Moving Speech

Mr. Hill used to tell the following humorous story of what he said on one occasion. "His Royal Highness, the Duke of—, was in the chair, and kindly desired me to sit next to him. A man spoke who absolutely had the bad taste to spin out his dull, tiresome oratory for more than an hour. Some of the people, tired to death, as well they might be, went away. His Royal Highness whispered to me, 'Really, Mr. Hill, I do not think I can sit to hear such another speech as this. I would like you to give one of your good-natured hints about it.'

"It was my turn to speak next, so I said, 'May it please your Royal Highness, ladies and gentlemen, I am not going to make either a long or a moving speech. The first is a rudeness, and the second is not required today. We have just heard a very moving speech – so moving that several of the company have been moved by it out of the room. I am afraid that another speech like that would so move his Royal Highness himself that he would be unable to continue in the chair and would, to the great regret of the meeting, be compelled to leave.' This delighted his Royal Highness, and we had no more long speeches that day."

An Apostolic Preacher

Dr. Stoughton said about Mr. Hill, "He was not learned, he was not logical in the scholastic acceptation of the term, he was not a rhetorician, and he was not a polished orator. Rather, he was rambling, diffuse, and unconnected, yet pointed, piercing, eminently evangelical, and thoroughly practical, and he wholeheartedly hated Antinomianism. In short, he was an apostolic preacher of the gospel."

A Providential Escape

When Rowland Hill was preaching at Devizes very early in his life, some fellow came to hear him with several snakes in his pocket. Watching his opportunity, he threw three at once at Mr. Hill. One coiled on his arm and another fastened on his neck. "Perceiving," he said, "that they were harmless, I merely took them off and threw them behind me, away from the crowd.

Some of the people immediately drove away the sinner, and the result was increased attention and several conversions to God. Soon afterward, the rebel came again to hear me, and he who would have alarmed me by serpents was himself rescued from the Old Serpent, and became for many years a steadfast follower of the Lamb of God."

Fruits of His Ministry

Mr. Hill was once attending the anniversary sermon for the London Missionary Society, at St. Bride's Church, when a most interesting circumstance occurred. The preacher was Dr. Gilbee, whose discourse from John 10:16 was full of piety and Christian love. Mr. Hill was so delighted that he said, "When I saw that he was concluding, I could hardly help crying out, 'Go on, Dr. Gilbee, please give us a little more of this good stuff.'" At the close of the service, he went to the vestry and, opening the door gently, asked permission to introduce himself.

"Dear Dr. Gilbee, will you permit a poor unworthy servant of our Divine Master to thank you for this day's sermon?"

"Oh, dearest Mr. Hill!" exclaimed Dr. Gilbee. "Come in, come in! How glad I am to see you! It was under your ministry that I was first led to God. I once wandered into your chapel. The music soothed me, and then and there it was I felt the power of the truth."

The Empty Napkin

A lady once requested him to examine her son as a candidate for the ministry, remarking, "I am sure he has a talent, but it is hid in a napkin."

At the end of the interview with the young man, Mr. Hill said, "Well, madam, I have shaken the napkin, and I cannot find the talent."

Diversion before Preaching

Rowland Hill was staying at a friend's house on one occasion, and retired, as the company supposed, to consider his sermon before preaching. However, when his host entered the room to inform him it was time to start, he found him with an old clock that he had taken apart. In response to the surprise that was expressed, he remarked, "I have been fixing your old clock, and I will finish it tomorrow." After this, he preached with more than usual ease and fervor, and drew several beautiful images from the activity in which his friend, to his surprise, had found him occupied.

The Story of the Pigs

Two friends once entered Surrey Chapel before going to India. One was a Christian, but the other was not. Mr. Hill preached from the text, *We are not ignorant of his devices* (2 Corinthians 2:11). He immediately told the following tale: "Many years ago I met a drove of pigs in one of the narrow streets of a large town, and to my surprise, they were not driven, but quietly followed their leader. This remarkable fact excited my curiosity, and I followed the swine until they all quietly entered the slaughterhouse. I then asked the man how he succeeded in getting the poor, stupid, stubborn pigs to follow him so willingly. He told me the secret. He had a basket of beans under his arm, and he kept dropping them as he proceeded, and so secured his object.

"Ah, my dear hearers, the devil has got his basket of beans, and he knows how to suit his temptations to every sinner. He drops them along the way, and the poor sinner is thus led captive by the devil at his will. If grace does not prevent it, Satan will get him at last into his slaughterhouse, and will keep him there forever. Oh, it is because *we are not ignorant of his devices* that we desire this evening to warn you against them."

The Christian friend mourned over this tale about the pigs, fearing that it would produce a smile, but would not produce conviction in the mind of his unbelieving companion. After the service they left the chapel, and all was silence for a season.

"What a strange story we heard tonight about the pigs, and yet how compelling and convincing it was," remarked the young man. His mind was affected. He could not forget the basket of beans, the slaughterhouse, and the final loss of the sinner's soul. He left this country, but soon after he corresponded with his friend and referred to this sermon as having produced a beneficial and, it is hoped, an abiding impression on his mind.

Order and Decorum

In the year 1798, Mr. Hill began his first tour in Scotland. At first, he had only a few small congregations, but after a few weeks, fifteen thousand people assembled to hear him on Calton Hill. A Scottish minister stated that he never heard an anecdote from a pulpit in his native land until Mr. Hill began his itinerant labors there.

The Scottish people complained that he rode upon all order and decorum. Mr. Hill, after this, called one of his carriage horses "Order" and the other "Decorum." When asked the reason, he answered, "Oh, I have given them these names so that the people in the north may tell the truth in one way if they do not in another, but I would be happy to ride on the back of such order and decorum as they advocate until I had ridden them to death."

An Expedient For Brevity

Mr. Hill once left London to promote the claims of Christian missions. He had not been feeling well, and promised to be brief in his sermons. A friend who was traveling with him kindly agreed to remind him when he forgot his promised limits. At Leeds, Hill addressed a great multitude in the Cloth Hall. He was excited by the scene and became inattentive to the gentle admonitions that he received by a pull at his coattail. After a while, he told the people what he had promised and how his brother had been pulling him by the coat. "Never mind," he added. "Let us have another pull, a strong pull, and a thorough pull, and who knows but that the devil's throne may fall from some poor sinner's heart?"

A Cheap Gospel

On going to preach at Bristol Tabernacle, he began his series of sermons on the eve of Bristol Fair. His text was Isaiah 55:1: *Ho, every one that thirsteth, come ye to the waters, and he that hath no money; come ye, buy and eat; yea, come, buy wine and milk without money and without price.* The congregation was large. He began with the following words: "My dear hearers, I guess many of you have come to attend Bristol Fair. So have I. You do not intend to show your goods until tomorrow, but I will display mine tonight. You are afraid that purchasers will not come up to your prices, but I am afraid that my buyers will not come down to mine, for mine," he said as he brought his hand down upon his Bible, "are *without money and without price.*"

Severe but Faithful

A rather talkative woman one day said to him, "I have spent a lot of time lately with some Roman Catholics, and they have sadly tempted me to change my religion."

"Indeed, ma'am," he replied, "I was not aware until now that you had any religion to change."

Toplady's Funeral Sermon

Mr. Augustus Toplady died on Tuesday, August 11, 1718, and on August 17, his remains were transported from Knightsbridge for interment in Tottenham Court Chapel. In accordance with his expressed desire that he might be laid in the sepulcher of the dead without any eulogy from the living, or the parade of an ostentatious funeral, the time of his burial was kept, as much as possible, concealed from the public. Still, from information that could not be prevented, thousands of people attended the ceremony, and Mr. Rowland Hill, unable to restrain the expression of his feelings, rose unexpectedly, and with an energy and pathos that commanded the breathless attention of the congregated multitude, delivered an unstudied, yet touching and beautiful, address on the excellences of him over whom they were then assembled to lament. The power of his language on this occasion added to his reputation as a speaker, and it also declared the real feeling and piety of his heart.

Preaching in Wales

It is said that wherever Mr. Hill went in Wales, he was followed by multitudes. He would seize the opportunity of the noontide rest from labor to gather around him the Welsh peasantry who live in the mountains, and on summer evenings thousands would congregate on the side of some romantic hill, after a walk of many miles by rugged and steep paths, to listen to his preaching. He could not speak Welsh, but the Welsh who understand English are exceedingly fond of hearing a sermon in the English language.

Personal Preaching

It is said of Rowland Hill that if you sat in the back seat in the gallery while he was preaching, you always had the idea that Mr. Hill was referring to you; or if you sat in the doorway where he could not see you, you were still quite convinced that he knew you were there and that he was preaching right at you.

The Atheist Reclaimed

A member of an atheist club came on a Sunday evening into Surrey Chapel merely to gratify his curiosity, or to ridicule the truths he heard, but returned home crying out for mercy and pardon. A few days later, he visited Mr. Rowland Hill to inquire what he must do to be saved. Although engaged in a laborious business, the former atheist dedicated his few leisure hours to the service of God, and it is thought that his benevolent exertions brought him to a premature, but happy, termination of his life.

Rejoicing with Trembling

One day Rowland Hill was talking with Mr. John Vine Hall, when the latter, speaking of some who profess to have attained a state of experience that forbids all fear, observed, "I am not there yet. I still rejoice with trembling." Mr. Hill replied, "Do not desire to get any further. Remember, blessed is the man that fears always (Proverbs 28:14). I am not afraid of the faithfulness of Christ, but I am afraid of the deceitfulness of my own heart."

An Earnest Wish

In the last sermon he ever preached, delivered on March 31, 1833, he said, "Oh, my dear brethren, I almost wish to be made young again, if I could only see such days as when I first came and preached at Tottenham Court Chapel and was in the habit of preaching in the streets and lanes for lack of room. Oh, how I love to think about what I then felt!"

Religion versus Worldliness

A member of Mr. Hill's congregation was in the habit of going to the theater. Mr. Hill went to him and said, "This will never do – a member of my church in the habit of attending the theater!" The man replied that it surely must be a mistake, as he was not in the habit of going there, although it was true he did go every once in a while for a treat.

"Oh," said Rowland Hill, "then you are a worse hypocrite than ever, sir. Suppose anyone spread the report that I ate carrion, and I answered, 'Well, there is no wrong in that; I don't eat carrion every day, but I have a little every once in a while for a treat!' Why, you would say, 'What a nasty, foul, and filthy appetite Rowland Hill has, to eat carrion for a treat!' The Christian religion is the Christian's genuine treat, and Christ is his enjoyment."

The Drunkard Saved

A drunkard, swearer, and cruel persecutor of his wife who belonged to Mr. Wesley's society received her one evening on her return from Rowland Hill's chapel with such kindness of manner that she was astonished. He said, "I have been to hear Mr. Hill. I am a sinner. You were right, and I was wrong. I hope I will never be unkind to you again, but that we will walk together in the same way."

Long Sermons

After Rowland Hill had reached his eighty-fourth year, it was not at all surprising that before he entered the pulpit, he would occasionally express a fear lest increasing weariness would cause him to preach with reduced force and effect. However, the wonder was that as soon as he began to address the people, this apprehension was entirely forgotten. Somebody might say to him at the close of the service, "Well, sir, notwithstanding your complaint of weakness, do you know how long you preached this morning?"

"Perhaps half an hour, or a little more."

"Why, sir, you were more than an hour in your sermon."

He then used to look astonished, and say, "Well, I am sure I did not have any idea of how long it was. It was too long for me, and too long for the people, but once I start going, I cannot stop. I must be shorter though."

Ministry to the Sick Poor

His attention to the little comforts of the afflicted poor made them feel that he really had their interests at heart. He was sometimes seen early in the summer searching his garden with a basket in his hand, looking for the few ripe strawberries he could find. He would then carry them to some sufferer to whom they would prove a welcome refreshment; and when he offered this little present, it was with a most affectionate kindness of manner.

Impatience of Restraints

In his old age, there were seasons when affliction kept him out of the pulpit, but it was necessary to keep a tender watch over him since there was danger of his moving off to the chapel as soon as he heard the distant notes of the organ. The evening of the new year was always a happy season with him, when the general communion of saints was enjoyed at Surrey Chapel. He was once confined with inflamed eyes, which were bound up. Most reluctantly, he agreed to remain at home – but just as the people were approaching the table of the Lord, the venerable man made his appearance. He had on a large blue cloak, and although blindfolded, he had found his way from the house into the chapel alone. The excitement produced cannot be described. There was a burst of affectionate feeling when the people saw their beloved pastor pressing toward the communion table, while the officiating ministers were urging him to return home. In the midst of this scene, he loudly exclaimed, "My dear people, they won't let me say one word to you." He then pronounced a brief but touching benediction upon them, and withdrew from the chapel.

Prescription for a Long Life

"Tell me, youngster," he said to a Sunday scholar, who afterward occupied his pulpit in Surrey Chapel (Dr. Stowell, of Rotherham College), "would you like to live long?"

"Yes, sir."

"Do you know how?"

"No, sir."

"Would you like me to tell you?"

"Please, sir."

"Work hard."

Number of Sermons Preached by Mr. Hill

From an account kept by Mr. Hill, it appears that up to June 10, 1831, he had preached 22,291 times. It may, therefore, be fairly concluded, that up to the close of his long ministry of sixty-six years, he had preached at least 23,000 sermons, being an average of nearly 350 every year. Many of these discourses were delivered in streets and fields. In reference to these services, Mr. Hill said that as far as he could determine, more souls were converted under those sermons than under any others that he preached. Other eminent ministers of the gospel have been equally diligent. George Whitefield, it appears, preached 18,000 sermons in thirty-four years, and John Wesley, who lived to about the same age as Mr. Hill, delivered 40,560 sermons.

An Apt Illustration

Preaching once in a manufacturing district, Mr. Hill said, "This evening, I watched the smoke arising from your factory chimneys, and although there was scarcely any air, yet how obediently it moved in the direction of the softest breeze. So it is with the Christian when God the Holy Spirit breathes upon his soul."

I Love Them Both Best

Rowland Hill was once preaching on the inseparable connection between justification and sanctification, when he thus concluded his remarks: "A person once asked a dear little child this improper question: 'Whom do you love best, your father or your mother?' The child paused for a moment, and then exclaimed, 'I love them both best.' If you ask me which I love best, justification or sanctification, I will answer with the little child, and never mind the bad grammar, 'I love them both best.'"

Spiritual Blindness

"I remember once being in company where a very fine child was present. He was very handsome, but he was blind, and he laughed at those who lamented that he was blind. If he had only once seen, he would have lamented his loss too! Let us once see the glory and grace of the gospel, and feel it applied to our hearts, and we will never forget its beauty."

Aversion

When preaching to very plain people, he said, "I want you to have a holy aversion to sin. Do you know what I mean by aversion? Suppose any of you were to put your hand into your pocket and feel a toad there. You would draw it out instantly from an aversion to the reptile. Do just so with regard to sin."

Sleepers Rebuked

Once at Wotton, he was preaching in the afternoon (the only time it seemed possible to be drowsy under him). He saw some people sleeping, and he paused, saying, "I have heard that the miller can sleep while the mill is going, but if it stops, it awakens him. I'll try this method." So he sat down, and soon saw an awakened audience.

Conscience – A Mirror

In a sermon at Surrey Chapel, he made a sharp address to young people about to be married. "You will have to get furniture," he said, "for your new home. Now there is one piece I would strongly recommend – a nice bright mirror – that is, a good conscience, which you should keep clean and clear so that you may see yourselves pleasantly reflected day by day."

Take Heed How You Hear

When making a tour in Yorkshire, an old man said to him, "Mr.

Hill, it has been sixty-five years since I first heard you preach, and I remember your text and part of your sermon."

"That is more than I do," was his reply.

"You told us," the old man proceeded, "that some people were very squeamish about the delivery of different ministers who preached the same gospel. You said, 'Suppose you were attending to hear a will read when you expected a legacy to be left to you. Would you use the time when it was being read to criticize the manner in which the lawyer read it? No, you would not. You would be giving all ear to him to hear if anything was left to you, and how much it was. That is the way I would advise you to hear the gospel.'"

Antinomianism

An Antinomian once called upon Mr. Hill in reference to his preaching a "legal gospel." When Rowland Hill asked him if he held "the Ten Commandments as a rule of life," the visitor replied, "Certainly not." Mr. Hill rang the bell, and when the servant made his appearance, he said, "Charles, show that man the door, and keep your eye on him until he is beyond the reach of every article of clothing or other property in the hall."

Idle Gossip Rebuked

On one occasion when Mr. and Mrs. Hill were visiting a friend in the country, the evening conversation turned upon a review of the characters of many personal friends and acquaintances. Mr. Hill remained a silent member of the group, and when he found that the verdicts pronounced were not in strict accordance with either truth or charity, he rose and rang the bell. The servant appeared, and he inquired if they had at hand a hearth brush and a dustpan. Being answered in the affirmative, he asked if he could use them for a few minutes. When they were brought in, he took them and began sweeping the carpet, saying that a large amount of dust and dirt had been scattered that evening, and he desired it to be removed. The hint was taken, and the conversation was directed to other topics.

Ingratitude

On one occasion, Rowland Hill offended the farmers of his congregation at Kingston by saying they were as bad as their pigs. When they demanded an explanation, he said, "Look at your pigs. When the acorns drop, they do not go under the elm tree in search for them, but under the oak; and when they have swallowed all they can find, off they go, without giving a single look at the tree that furnished their meal. So you, like your pigs, know where to go to look for your wheat, and when your barns are filled with plenty, like them, you forget to look up to the Source from whom all your blessings have been obtained."

Rowland Hill's Ferrets

Soon after the opening of Surrey Chapel, several devoted men went through the crowded districts of Southwark talking to the poor and holding district meetings for prayer. There were people who considered these proceedings irregular, and they complained to Mr. Hill about it. "Let them alone," said the good pastor. "They are my ferrets; they go into the holes and corners where I cannot go, and they drive out the poor sinner to hear the gospel."

Part 3

Pulpit Sayings and Illustrations

Chapter 7

Pulpit Sayings and Illustrations

Reciprocity

The grace that leads to Christ previously comes from Christ. If I live *on* Him, I feel that I am enabled to live *to* Him. There is nothing that will teach me to live above the world except living upon Christ.

Let us always look to God to implant the principle, and then we may depend upon it that we will abound in the practice.

As soon as I am brought under the blessed influence of the life of God, every heartbeat will be to His glory.

The Robe of Righteousness

Although I am imperfect in myself, there is a word that tells me I am complete in Christ. The redemption is completely worked out. The righteousness that is unto all, and upon all those who believe, is a robe of which it is truly said "no age can change its glorious hue,"[12] but it will be our everlasting ornament in the mansions of glory.

My dear Savior has not only provided for me pardoning

---

12 This is a line from a hymn that begins with "God's Christ, who is my righteousness," written by Nicolaus Zinzendorf (1700-1760) and translated by John Wesley (1703-1791).

love, but renewing grace. Nine-tenths of a believer's prayer is for purity of heart.

The Devil's Curiosities

What is to be done with those professors of religion who are half for Baal and half for God? They know so much of religion that they are spoiled for the world. They do not go very often to the theater, only now and then as a curiosity. May God keep us from the devil's curiosities! Do all who come to the Lord's Table prove themselves to be what they should be? I wish they did! I think if the devil could pick out from among the people of God those who belong to him, he would have a pretty good selection. If I am not fit for earthly communion, am I fit for the communion above?

I have an idea of what heaven is above when I feel heaven upon earth. Glorification is a completion of the work of grace.

A Preacher's Ambition

I see many of my juniors called away before me into an eternal world. I pray that when my time comes (and that must now be near), I may die with an honest pulpit conscience that I have preached the truth from my heart.

Do not strive to make yourselves holy by working, but by believing, by living out of yourselves and entirely on the strength of Christ. The believer's life is a life *hid with Christ in God* (Colossians 3:3).

The Blessing of Affliction

The children of God should never look upon afflictions as sent in anger, but as merciful visitations – for whom the Lord loveth,

He chastens (Hebrews 12:6). Every twig of His rod grows in the paradise of His love. Let your afflictions have the tendency to move you to prayer. A child of God in an imprisoned state of affliction is far better off than sinners at liberty.

I am told of *the beauty of holiness* (Psalm 96:9). There is infinite beauty in the holiness of God. We are beautified when we are made holy.

Free Pardon

I must have a more enlarged mind for a better world. I must have a bigger vessel for bigger joys. As much of a sinner as I am, I have no more sins to answer for than if I were an angel, for my Savior has paid the uttermost farthing. If we had even one sin to answer for, we must lose heaven.

The work of spiritual religion is entirely the work of the Holy Spirit. It is as much beyond our reach, naturally, as the stars in the firmament.

Blessings of Repentance

My God, let me have that repentance that is only to be learned by living near You.

No one knows how to pray for conversion until he is converted.

Repentance is the handmaid that is sent to scour our hearts; then the Lord comes to dwell in them.

I am an old man, and must soon be done with preaching. It will not do for me to talk about trifles just to please the ear. I do no good here unless I do good to your souls while you are here. It is better to gain one soul to Christ than to gain the admiration of thousands.

The Covenant of Grace

We know nothing of the covenant of grace except as we feel the grace of the covenant in our hearts. There is a holy impossibility that where grace reigns, sin can reign also. They who live under fleshly principles cannot please God. It is fitting that infinite holiness should love its own image wherever He implants it; as vile as you are, He has made you lovely by His grace.

God creates in me an appetite for Himself, and He is the Bread of Life to satisfy that appetite.

Grace and Works

If grace works in us, we cannot stop working for God any more than we can stop breathing. When the heart is right, everything else will be right.

Happy are they who are enabled to devote their early life to God!

Hear with astonishment the large charter of blessings promised: *all things are yours* (1 Corinthians 3:21)!

Angels

I do not know them, but I will know them hereafter. We will be the surprise of angels that God could make creatures who were so averse to all good the inheritors of His kingdom.

Peter seemed the boldest of all the disciples, but there was something at the core that he could not see, and when he was tried, it came out. May God Almighty save us from self-confidence.

The New Creation

Carnal men may say prayers, but they cannot pray. It is natural for man to fear wrath, but it is supernatural in man to love holiness. We know nothing of life until we are born, and we know nothing of spiritual life until we are born again.

There will be no cry to be saved until the beginning of salvation has created that cry in our hearts.

If mankind is left to their own laws and ways, they are very devils; but if Christ takes them in hand (for instance, look at the South Sea Islands), His very name will pray away their iniquities.

Meditation

There is nothing more glorious to meditate upon than the infinite dignity and majesty of Christ. May God enlarge our hearts so that we may receive more from Him, and may He make us to hunger and thirst more after Him. It is the sweetest thing in the world to be overwhelmed with gratitude toward Him.

Holy Courage

Come, beloved, and magnify our glorious King by calling down His mighty power for vengeance on your sins. Don't be a coward; remember, holy courage is a heavenly virtue. The great work of Christ is to destroy the work of the devil. The more we know of Christ, the more we will hate sin, for it is sin alone that keeps us from Him.

Poverty of spirit is the bag into which Christ puts the riches of His grace.

Strength in Weakness

Don't look after the power in yourselves, but expect the power of God to rest upon you. May the Lord make you know that you have nothing in yourselves. The basis of real humility is a knowledge of ourselves, feeling that we can do nothing without God.

The apostle James says, *Count it all joy when ye fall into divers temptations* (James 1:2). I do not want Satan to tempt me, but if I am tempted, let it be a matter of thankfulness that I am enabled to resist by looking up to God for momentary strength.

Be Reconciled to God

Be ye reconciled to God (2 Corinthians 5:20). The best of God's people have enough to lament before Him. Be careful not to quarrel with God. Let Him alone, and be content to be at His disposal. Pray for a yielding spirit, a childlike acceptance, when anything tries your patience.

There is that in Christ that my best notions can never reach.

Sense of Shortcoming

Nothing sets us right as much as a sense of our shortcomings before God. Do you love God more, or pray to Him more, than you should? Examine yourselves, and blush for shame (Ezra 9:6). It is strange that we would try to tell God what to do, yet there is often a great deal of this in our proud hearts. There is not a more beautiful metaphor than the clay and the potter (Isaiah 29:16; 64:8). Oh, yield to every touch of God's providence. Remember that you are nothing but ignorance and folly, and all that is wise and good comes from God, and from God alone.

The Dignity of the Redeemed

How much we are dignified by regeneration! Your bodies are the temples of the Holy Spirit (1 Corinthians 6:19)! We should strive to act, walk, and speak as such. The most important matter should not be what man thinks of us, but what God thinks of us. The praise of man is only a distasteful indication that we are not ready for the praise of God.

We can never partake of Christ, the heavenly Bread, without a heavenly effect. If I live upon that wholesome Bread, I will be happy.

An Alternative

I question whether there is a moment in which we are not either sinning or, in some way or other, bringing forth fruit to the glory of God.

Are some of you causing joy to the angels of God because you are coming to the God of angels? Do you desire to be right with God? A man can never be sent to hell with right desires.

Strength for Victory

When the enemy comes to drive you down from that high hill of holiness that you should possess, fall down awhile, and while you are down, let your heart be up to God. When He gives the word of command, "Stand up; let Israel go forward" (Exodus 14:15), then fight manfully, for the victory is sure.

Christian Evidence

If I could see my name written in the brightest colors in the Lamb's Book of Life, I would not take that as so good an evidence as having His lovely law written and engraved on my heart (Jeremiah 31:33).

We Are Debtors

I truly believe that if you try to be as good as you should be, you will find yourselves much worse than you think. There would be no more good in the best of you than there is in hell if God did not put it there. If God leaves the best of men to themselves, they will soon act as the worst. *We are debtors, not to the flesh, to live after the flesh. For if ye live after the flesh, ye shall die: but if ye through the Spirit do mortify the deeds of the body, ye shall live* (Romans 8:12-13).

Look at Christ until you are conformed to His image. Look to Him that you may know more of Him.

The Shield of Faith

Keep the shield of faith constantly before an upright heart. Then let Satan's darts come by the millions; down they will fall, and you will triumph gloriously. You may go into heaven without your shield, but you must carry it to heaven's door.

How compassionately Christ clothed Himself in our humanity and feelings! He had all human compassion, as well as divine omnipotence.

The Guest of the Heart

Ye are not your own (1 Corinthians 6:19). Your bodies are the temples of the Holy Spirit. Is that an unmeaning metaphor or an overworded expression? When God enters the soul, heaven enters with Him. The heart is compared to a temple. God never enters without His attendants. Repentance cleanses the house. Faith provides for the house. Watchfulness, like the porter, takes care of it. Prayer is a lively messenger. Prayer learns what is needed and then seeks to obtain it. Faith tells him where to go, and he never goes in vain.

Joy is the musician of this temple, tuning to the praises of God and the Lamb. This terrestrial temple will be removed to the celestial world, for the trumpet will sound, and the dead will be raised (1 Corinthians 15:52).

He who reigns to bring us to heaven will in time reign to keep us there forever.

Repentance – A Grace

Repentance! When God sends that nice, lively, active grace into the heart, what a diligent search it makes to cleanse out every sin! Repentance is not the work of the Law, but it is a grace of the gospel.

In prayer, never let me be satisfied without the supply of all my needs. The best way to have our needs provided for is to look into our Bibles and see what we should need, then see what is provided for us there, and then go to God for a manifestation of His power.

The Law is a mirror, not to make me beautiful, but to show me my deformities.

As vile and deformed by sin as I once was, yet when adorned with His lovely likeness, God Himself delights in me.

Election and Sanctification

We have no right to judge of election except by sanctification. How do I know that I am chosen of God? I know by God being my choice. I am to judge of my election by the habit of sanctification, that I am steadily and perseveringly holy. That is what we want to feel in time – a heaven of holiness.

God Himself cannot make me happy without making me holy. I am only happy as God makes me holy. A Christian's obedience is straightforward work.

The Blessing of Afflictions

We will have to bless God for the storm that heaves us, wave after wave, into the harbor of eternal rest. We will have more to do to bless God for what He denies us than for what He gives us. Let the Lord choose my lot, and let me be content with it.

God be praised, for the old man has a dying life in a living Christian.

A Peculiar People

When I was young, my friends wrote to me and told me not to make myself peculiar. I don't want to make myself peculiar, but I hope God will make me peculiar by making me peculiarly holy. May the divine image be restored to me so that I may be what I should be.

Your life is hid with Christ in God (Colossians 3:3). The world cannot see it in principle, so let them see it in practice.

The New Year

We are beginning a new year; begin well with Christ. Perhaps the reason I don't preach better is because you do not pray more; and the reason you do not profit more is because you do not pray enough for a blessing. I feel it is important work to preach, and may you feel that it is important work to hear. May you begin, continue, and end this year with God.

I am to be perpetually full of needs so that I may be perpetually receiving out of the fullness of Christ Jesus my Lord.

Repentance – A Constant Grace

There were three thousand pricked to the heart (Acts 2:37). These were the firstfruits. When they heard that Christ had been wounded for their transgressions, they were pricked to the heart. This produced repentance. I tell every repentant person not to be content with his share of repentance, but to pray that it may sink deeper and deeper into his heart. If you continue in the practice of repentance, you will not commit sin.

A Christian does not work for God like pumping a well that ceases when the hand stops pumping, but it is like a spring that is always flowing.

Triumph over Sin

If sin attacks you, attack sin by believing. You have a Bible that tells you, *We are more than conquerors* (Romans 8:37). Do you say sin is too strong for you? It is not too strong for Omnipotence who dwells in you.

I don't want to be afraid of going to hell. I want to be afraid of sin. Let me be afraid of sin, and then I do not need to be afraid of going to hell.

Family Religion

It is the solemn duty of every Christian head of a family to remember that the care of his family's souls is committed to his charge. Family religion is of essential consequence.

How to Die

Where you die, when you die, or by what means you die is scarcely worth a thought if you simply die in Christ.

Lights of the World

It is not the position in life that we fill that is as important as the light we send forth from it. Thanks be to God, we may glorify Him in our various roles more than we might imagine. There is no condition, however humble, that prevents the zealous Christian from doing something to the honor and praise of his God.

Away with your frozen divinity. It will never do for us who desire to be warmed with divine love.

Life in Christ

When we are risen with Christ, we leave the grave of our corruption and rise up to newness of life. If I am risen with my living Head, I must live by my Head.

The Lord makes that which is lovely, and then loves that which is made lovely.

The Rod of Affliction

Nothing is by blind chance. Everything is under the management of infinite wisdom. I would therefore take all things as coming from God so that they may lead me to God. The rod of affliction that He uses is made up of many twigs, but they are all cut from the same tree.

While repentance views the justice of God, faith looks up and sees the scepter of mercy.

Unity in Diversity

We have heard before now of such a strong family likeness that it was hard to distinguish between two individuals of the same family. And there is a wonderful likeness among the children of God. We do wiser and better to look after that than to look after the petty denominations and ways into which Christianity is now too much divided. There is but one and the same grace belonging to them all. God be praised, all these minor differences that prevail so much in time will cease when we come to see as we are seen, know as we are known, and come to be forever with the Lord.

Wise Correction

We should chastise our children as the Lord corrects His: never in wrath, but always in love. Every stripe given by an angry hand or from a revengeful heart increases the evil for which the child is so unwisely and unmercifully corrected.

I want to feel a holy tendency to give my heart to God and to walk in His ways; I do believe I will go to heaven if I have heaven in my heart now.

True Faith

True faith, like the dove sent forth by Noah, may hover over the waters for a season without finding a resting-place, but will always return to the ark bearing the olive branch of peace and love.

A person may have as many religious changes in the year as there are changes in the moon, yet remain unchanged.

Shadow and Substance

The outward form of religion is one thing, and its substance another. I have heard of a person who wanted to be dressed very fine in his coffin, but would that restore life? The Comforter is sent to us for the very purpose that He may put spiritual life within us.

We are called to self-denial so that we may be kept from denying Christ.

The Preparation of the Heart

We know with what excellent detail the skillful engraver can represent the forms he produces, but it is essential to his art that the substance he engraves upon is suited to receive the impression. What could he do on the surface of a coarse tile? In the same way, God refines the heart to prepare it to receive His lovely image. Then, by the operation of His Spirit, He completes the glorious work.

Prisoners Set Free by Christ

Genuine repentance will drive us from sin to Christ, and the Bible reveals no other salvation but through Him. Just as prisoners can never open their prison doors by the deepest repentance for their crimes, so no acquittal from the wickedness of our sins can ever be obtained except through the sufferings and death of Christ, who opens the prison doors to those who are firmly tied and bound with the chains of their sins.

True Religion

It is true religion itself that explains itself to the happy soul that has it. May God give you that religion in your hearts that explains itself by itself and enables you to set to your seal that God is true.

The Divine Father

In all the pursuits of time, the child of God will never lose sight of his heavenly Father. I have often seen a little child following his parent in the fields, stooping now and then to gather a few flowers. He looks up and sees him at a distance, and the little creature runs and catches up to him again, afraid that he might go too far away. So the Christian, while gathering a few flowers from the world, allows his God to be often at a distance from him; but the instant he realizes that he is alone, he runs to reach again his Father, Protector, and Friend.

Fears

I would not have you suppose that all your fears are ungodly fears; there is no harm in having a suspicion of ourselves. We should examine ourselves, as Satan is very busy in his attacks.

Flowers and Fruit

I love to see all the flowers and fruit that God makes the earth bring forth to please us, and then I think, "Oh, that I could bear more fruit of righteousness to please Him!"

Feeling

There cannot be true religion without feeling. How can you pray without feeling your needs? How can you fear without feeling your danger? How can you love without feeling that the object of your love is lovely? If you cry out, "Oh, the remains of my corruptions," cry on. God loves to hear such cries.

Love Is All

If the sun shines on dull bricks or stones, they reflect none of its beams, for there is nothing in them capable of this. Nor is there in an ungodly man any natural power of reflecting the light of God. However, let the sun shine upon a diamond, and see what rays of sparkling beauty it emits. In the same way, the Christian who has the graces of the Spirit reflects beams of celestial loveliness upon the world when God shines in his soul.

The Christian's character should savor of holiness. The promise is, *I will be as the dew unto Israel* (Hosea 14:5), and how sweet is the fragrance of the flower after the gentle falling of the dew! So must the true believer be under the soft rain of the droppings of heaven on his heart. Cultivate a spirit of love. Love is the diamond among the jewels of a believer's breastplate. The other graces shine like the precious stones of nature, with their own peculiar luster and various hues, but the diamond is white. In white, all the colors are united, and so in love is centered all the other Christian graces and virtues.

There is nothing like the shower of pardoning love to water the soil so that grace may grow.

The Blindness of Ignorance

Ignorant minds may struggle and wander about because they know nothing of the truth, but to those whose minds are enlightened from above, all will appear as brilliance itself. I may take a man out on a fine starlit night and, pointing to a star of the first brilliancy and magnitude, I may say, "Do you see that beautiful star?" and he says, "No, I do not." Why, how is this? The man is blind.

We cannot shine with rays of our own, but we must shine if shined upon.

The Perfect Law

Observe the plumage of some elegant bird. Mark accurately the smallest part of its varied adornment, and see whether you can note a single defect in its Maker's skillful work. Thus, the most detailed regulations of the law of God prove the perfect wisdom of the infinite mind that framed and gave the whole.

God forbid that I should say my holiness is my merit, but it is my mercy.

The Clearness of Essential Truths

Scripture is like the firmament on a fine starlit night. Many bright spheres are set in the midst of much obscurity. Thanks be to God, though, that the parts necessary to be seen by me are luminous. There is not in the Bible a single essential truth that is not comparatively plain.

Conformity to the World

In all ages, conformity to the world has proved to be the ruin of the church. It is utterly impossible to live in nearness to God and in friendship with the world.

The Love of God that Passes Knowledge

I am unable to reach the lofty theme of the love of God, yet I do not think that the child who swims in the mighty ocean ever complains that there is too much water for him to swim in. So it is with me. I may be permitted, with my little childlike powers, to plunge into a subject I will never be fully able to comprehend.

Zeal in Prayer

I do not repent that I pray, but I do repent that I do not pray with more zeal.

Light Is Its Own Revealer

All the lights in the world put together will not show the sun. The sun is only to be seen by its own effects. So the Sun of Righteousness is only to be seen by human eyes, as the fullness and brightness of the Father's glory, by the light that guides His people to Himself.

The Bible Is True

The Bible, while it has so many wise things in it, could not have been the composition of fools or of bad men, as the design of it is entirely to counteract the corrupt morals and bad principles of the world and to instill that which is excellent and good. It could not have been composed by deceitful men, for it was composed by many different penmen at such different ages of the world.

Remedy for Sin

May God bring you to the only remedy against that dreadful disease of sin. The poor sinner who speaks to you from the pulpit found it at the foot of the cross.

The Bible's Beauty and Strength

Oh, the simplicity, the energy, the beauty of the language of the Bible – the spiritual language of God the Holy Spirit! The longer I live in the world, and the more I read my Bible, the more I am amazed at the immeasurable power of the Bible – the glorious strength of its phraseology – so far beyond anything that is human.

I remember when I was at the university many years ago that there was one who pretended to have great wisdom and to have wonderful insight into the things of God. He could not, he said, see the wonderful passages some were so fond of. I pointed out that passage, *When Christ, who is our life, shall appear, then shall ye also appear with Him in glory* (Colossians 3:4). But what is meant by Christ being the life of the soul? The dead can know nothing of life, nor can those who have not been made partakers of divine life comprehend the beauty of those passages that speak of its nature and effects.

Saved

I am saved by the Father in a way of providence, I am saved by the Son in a way of redemption, and I am saved by the Spirit in a way of regeneration.

God's Hatred of Sin

I can no more explain the infinite hatred of God to sin than I can tell you the height of the heavens above. Infinite holiness must have an infinite hatred against everything that is unholy. God's heaven is Himself, and His own happiness is His own eternal and essential holiness. If God could be deprived of this, He would cease to be happy.

The Divine Decree

When God says, *Let there be light* (Genesis 1:3), is it in the power of all hell to create darkness? When He says, *Arise, shine* (Isaiah 60:1), will not Omnipotence prevail? We triumph while we believe in God. *If God be for us, who can be against us?* (Romans 8:31).

Christ All in All

I have often admired the sweet repetition, if it may be called that, of the precious name of Jesus throughout the whole of Paul's epistles, wherein he can hardly write a single line without mentioning and exalting the Lord Christ as the believing sinner's all in all.

Full Redemption

Jesus has *put away sin by the sacrifice of Himself* (Hebrews 9:26). You do not need to fear the penalties of the curse while you view Christ crucified as the object of your faith and make Him the only plea for your acceptance before God. Never before was justice so magnified nor mercy so plainly revealed. If the Creator had delivered up a thousand angels, that would not have been a sacrifice anywhere near equal to that of His not even sparing His well-beloved Son when He stood as man for men to bear the vengeance of His wrath. Oh, the justice that demanded such an atonement! Oh, the mercy that revealed such a salvation for a ruined world! Can sinners hear of such mercy and resist it – sinners doomed to die for sins more in number than the sands on the seashore? Oh, what callous hearts must those be that can be proof against such astonishing love, yet refuse to yield themselves to Him who paid so great a price for sinners so worthless and so vile!

Pride Rooted Out

The person who loves his garden will not allow the weeds to grow in it. The weed of pride is in our hearts, and God will root it out.

Unsearchable Riches

Who can speak properly of the blessings included in the unsearchable riches of Christ? That is a fine passage, *Eye hath not seen, nor ear heard, neither have entered into the heart of man the things that God hath prepared for them that love Him* (1 Corinthians 2:9). The eye has seen great things. On a clear night, for example, how much, and to what an immense distance, the eye can behold! With those wonderful telescopes, how much farther it can penetrate! My thoughts can penetrate farther than my eyes can see or my ears can hear, but the eye cannot see all, nor the ear hear all, nor the heart conceive all. Neither can we hear, or even properly realize, all of the unsearchable riches of Christ. Oh, let us meditate more on the great things that God has laid up for those who love Him.

Rise above Your Corruptions

If you want to get above your doubts and fears, get above your corruptions; sin feeds unbelief.

Christ – The Alpha and Omega

Christ crucified may be said to be the Alpha and Omega of all the Bible. There is not a promise given that does not refer to Him. There is not a warning or judgment pronounced where He is not represented as a shelter from the storm and a refuge for the guilty. Not a prophecy is revealed in which the testimony of Jesus is not the spirit of prophecy. Not one priestly institution was ever ordained, not one bleeding bullock or slaughtered lamb ever stained a Jewish altar, except what was meant to represent a crucified Redeemer as the Lamb of God, *slain from the foundation of the world* (Revelation 13:8).

All the lives of the patriarchs, filled with unusual and

instructive providences, demonstrate the fullness of God's grace. While we pleasingly read of the tenderness of a forgiving Joseph to his returning brethren, the meekness of a Moses, the strength of a Samson, the patience of a Job, and the wisdom of a Solomon, at once we see all their excellent qualities as faint representations of Him in whom dwells *all the fullness of the Godhead bodily* (Colossians 2:9); of Him who stands as the Creator of each inferior star while shining forth with His own innate glories as the Sun of righteousness (Malachi 4:2). He appears as the only light in a dark world. Without this light, how great would our darkness be!

The Everlasting Covenant

God did not enter into the covenant of grace with man in a fallen state. It never can be admitted that God, the Eternal Sovereign, could enter into such a covenant with a set of rebels. The covenant was not made between God and fallen man, but between God the Father and God the Son, even the Man Christ Jesus, the second Adam, the Lord from heaven, who became the Substitute for our sinful race. To give it directly in biblical language, He became *the surety of a better testament* (Hebrews 7:22), or the *mediator of the new testament* (Hebrews 9:15), established upon better promises.

Stand Firm

When we are afraid and begin to retreat, the devil knows he is gaining ground. I cannot bear running away and turning my back; there is no armour given for the back.

No Happiness without Jesus

You cannot be happy while you live, you cannot be happy when you die, and you cannot be happy in eternity unless you go to the blessed Jesus to save your precious soul. Why would you wait? What sin can be as lovely as the love of Christ? Oh, think of this, and let me, as your sincere friend, plead with you to turn and live. Live to God now, and you will live with Him to all eternity!

Man, His Own Enemy

We have a terrible enemy in Satan, but we have one still worse in our own sinful hearts. I defy the foe without if I am not likely to be betrayed by the foe within.

Hatred of Sin

The Holy Spirit first enlightens us, and then makes us abhor sin as detestable and abhorrent. No child of God, no heir of heaven, can love sin or live in it. He groans under it and looks on the right hand and on the left for a way of escape. Just as I can never submit my flesh to allow a hot burning coal to be applied to it, so, if I am a child of God, I can never be reconciled to the power of sin in my soul.

The Root of Superstition

Where there is only a little real religion, the lack of it is too frequently supplied by an abundance of error. The human mind tends to run into extremes on every occasion. Some believe too much, and others believe too little. Happy are those who, being blessed with that *wisdom that is from above* (James 3:17), are preserved in the middle path and are saved from every extreme.

Love – A Holy Grace

The repentance that is most genuine is that which springs from love. We can never willingly offend where we sincerely love. Love is that holy grace that fills us with a godly jealousy over ourselves.

Heaven Begun Below

Righteousness creates a heaven in every man's house into which it enters, and it becomes the glory of the family circle.

The Benevolence of Religion

I want a religion that is good, and one that will do me good because it is good. When people talk about their religion, they should not be ashamed to have these questions asked to them: "What has your religion done for you? What effect has it produced upon your mind? What influence has it exerted on your attitude and on your conduct?"

We preach a religion that makes us new creatures in Christ Jesus (2 Corinthians 5:17), that makes us partakers *of the divine nature* (2 Peter 1:4); and that destroys the old man and makes us anew, creating us *in righteousness and true holiness* (Ephesians 4:24). This must be of God alone. The highest archangel in heaven cannot create a worm of the earth nor give existence to the lowest reptile.

Saved and Restored

The gospel not only saves me from the damnation I deserve, but it restores me to the divine image.

Justification and Good Works

Faith and repentance are the effects of our salvation. They cannot, therefore, be the cause of it any more than motion, which is the effect of life, can be said to be the cause of why we live or move. Bishop Beveridge settles the matter: "How can I do good works in order to be justified when I cannot do good works until after I am justified?"

Christian Morality

The morality of our Lord's Sermon on the Mount amounts to this – that the real Christian is dead to every vile passion and is most completely devoted to God.

Redemption and Its Effects

While a minister preaches redemption by Christ, unless he also shows the glorious effects of this redemption, he tells you of a treasure chest without a jewel, or sets before you a fine picture he drew that leads you to admire his ability, though it gives you but little idea of life. I remember once talking with a celebrated sculptor who had been hewing out of a block of marble a representation of one of our great patriots, Lord Chatham. "There," he said. "Is not that a fine figure?"

"Now, sir," I replied, "can you put life into it? Else, with all its beauty, it is still only a block of marble." Christ by His Spirit, however, puts life into a pleasing image, and then enables the man He forms to live to His praise and glory.

The Believer's Sunset

Do you see how majestically and brightly the sun sheds its parting rays around you? I have heard that the rays of the setting sun produce a most beneficial effect on the vegetable world. Oh, that my setting sun, which must soon go down in death, may during the evening of my days be more and more blessed in shedding a beneficial light on the trees the Lord has planted and is watering to His glory!

Breath

Your breath is in your nostrils, and you must breathe your last as well as your first breath – and soon your last breath will come.

Jesus Only

Lord, to whom shall we go? (John 6:68) To the law that curses us? To the world that is a delusive bubble? To sin and corruption that has polluted our minds and caused us trouble in abundance. Where can we go? *Thou hast the words of eternal life.* We know and are sure that You are *the Christ, the Son of the living God* (Matthew 16:16).

The Church Broader than the Sects

God has His people among all denominations of Christians, but none of them are any better for being devoted to their denomination. I will leave you to follow your own group, but I will not leave you because you are not of my group. I want to love the image of God wherever I find it, in preference to any denomination or group.

Monsters – Made By Sin

Sin turns people into monsters, rendering them *implacable, unmerciful, and without natural affection* (Romans 1:31). The gospel, on the other hand, turns monsters into men, directing them to be gentle and merciful among themselves, and to bless their very persecutors.

The Heart versus Brains

I have heard many people cry out, "Your religion is too strict for us; your manner of preaching will not do for our way of living." I see, therefore, that it is of little use to instruct people's heads until God has set their hearts right. They become right in judgment by God making them right in heart.

Like Loves Like

It is an old proverb that "Like loves like, all the world over." This is fully exemplified among the children of God, where they have right feelings and where the communion of saints lovingly prevails. When we truly love God, we are sure to love one another.

Looking Up

People talk about looking back on a well-spent life. I look up to Him who spent His life gloriously to redeem the life of my precious soul, and there alone I dare to look. I thank God, who has kept me from the more offensive sins of the world, but there is not a prayer more suitable to my dying lips than that of the publican: *God be merciful to me a sinner* (Luke 18:13).

Different Styles of Preaching

Careless preaching displeases. Weak preaching does nothing but leave poor souls fast asleep. Bold preaching, though, if delivered under an affectionate love to the souls of men and with a humble desire to promote the glory of God, is the only preaching that is loved and blessed of Him.

Submission

We can never desire to say, *Thy will be done* (Matthew 6:10) until the kingdom of God is set up in our hearts, and we can have no evidence that the kingdom of God is within us unless we produce *righteousness, peace, and joy in the Holy Ghost* (Romans 14:17).

Pray without Ceasing

The Christian is told to *pray without ceasing* (1 Thessalonians 5:17). It is not that he can always be engaged in the positive act, but he should have what I call a holy aptitude for prayer. The bird is not always in the air, but he is ready to fly in an instant. So the believer is not always engaged in the act of praying, but he has such a gracious aptitude for this exercise that he is prepared in an instant, when in danger or need, to run to his God for refuge.

Places of Prayer

I would not want to be found anywhere where prayer would be inconsistent. I cannot pray at a horserace or at a theater; and who, we ask the question, would like to spend his last breath in a theater?

Character – A Good Preacher

That man is a bad preacher in the pulpit who is not a good preacher out of it. No man in the world has a right to stand up for God if God has not adorned him with personal holiness. We should preach by what we are, as well as by what we say.

The Believer's Armor

The believer never turns his back on his enemy. Christian, show your shining breastplate of righteousness. Go forward and advance toward your enemy, and God will protect you behind. He has promised it: *The glory of the* LORD *shall be thy reward* (Isaiah 58:8).

Division – The Devil's Wedge

What sort of an evil is a partisan and denominational spirit? It is the cruel iron wedge of the devil's own forging that is used to separate Christians from each other. Christians thereby become like divided armies.

Hatred of Sin – The Work of Grace

In the person who is born of the Spirit, the grace of God produces a natural hatred to sin, even though he loved it in his old condition. The vulture's nature is to prey, with horrid preference, on the rotten carcasses of the dead. But did you ever see the gentle dove gorging on this loathsome food? In the same way, the sinner feeds with delight on the nauseous enjoyments of his iniquity, like the carrion-eating bird of prey, while the regenerate soul has a holy disgust of all that is offensive to its heavenly nature.

Sermons

I do not think that sermon is worth anything that does not have the Redeemer in it.

Dreams Not Trustworthy

A man once applied to be admitted to the sacrament at Surrey Chapel. He stated that his religious feelings originated in a dream. "Well, that may be," said Mr. Hill, "but we'll tell you what we think of your dreams when we have seen how you walk now that you are awake."

Walking with God

Seek to have God with you in your daily walk. Get Him into your families, and keep Him there. What a happy sight it is to see parents ruling at the head of the family in the fear of God, and how delightful to see the children brought up *in the nurture and admonition of the Lord* (Ephesians 6:4)!

Humility

May the Lord keep us from pride as we always remember that we are followers of the humble and lowly Jesus (Matthew 11:29). It is very improper to see the servant proud and the master humble. You will never get good while your hearts are lifted up with pride.

Holy Delicacy of Mind

The people of the world want a religion that will accept them in sin. They want to compromise matters with God. However, we are commanded to come out from the world and not to touch the unclean thing (2 Corinthians 6:17). May God give us that holy sensitivity of mind that will cause us to *abstain from all appearance of evil* (1 Thessalonians 5:22).

Provision for the Way

Yours may be a rough way through the wilderness, but God will not allow you to be tempted *above that you are able* (?). We may travel on in the gospel chariot, not only without cost, but God also provides heavenly provision for all the sacred pilgrims.

God – The Source of All Good

The ground produces nothing of itself without a blessing upon it. It is the same with the heart. God is the fountain of all good. I must get God to get good. I have no thought of anything doing me good except as it brings me near God.

Marching Order

With dignity and holy courage, let us march in the heavenly way. As long as the captain of our salvation goes before us (Hebrews 2:10), and the grace of Christ is in us, what do we have to fear? How can I not be sure of victory with such a Victorious One to support me?

Prayer – The Secret of Security

You never read God's Word profitably except as it teaches you to pray while you read. I go nowhere in a spirit of safety except as I go in a spirit of prayer.

We Know Not What We Will Be

What will my mind be two hundred thousand years from now when I will have been growing all the time? God forbid that we should neglect our souls and think them to be insignificant when they will be enlarging and increasing in knowledge to all eternity! Don't degrade yourselves. As little as you are now in knowledge, you are to grow eternally.

Be Careful for Nothing

Be careful for nothing; but in every thing by prayer and supplication with thanksgiving let your requests be made known unto God (Philippians 4:6). The Lord cares for the righteous. He knows all their sorrows. You and I are very ignorant creatures. We do not know how much care we need.

Remember, you can't have your souls in kinder hands. God knows what you need. Our dear Physician knows precisely what is best. Be quiet and content, then. Don't direct Him, but let Him direct you. This is the way the people of God learn righteousness.

Understanding and Memory

I know that my Redeemer liveth (Job 19:25). It is amazing what a blessing the understanding is. This is the repository, like a warehouse, to deposit your goods. Then comes the memory to remember what is past, and reflection to consider what we are doing.

The Redeemer – One with Us

He who used to act the part of a redeemer was one of near kin. We bless God our Redeemer, who has taken upon Himself our nature, and is bone of our bone and flesh of our flesh. This is a fine expression: my Redeemer – from sin and all its vile effects. If Christ takes possession of my heart, I expect by redemption just what that passage says: He came to *redeem us from all iniquity, and to purify unto Himself a peculiar people, zealous of good works* (Titus 2:14).

Not on Your Own

Never attempt one duty without God, but you may attempt ten thousand with Him.

In Heavenly Places

Oh, it was a glorious day when our Lord had all His disciples together, and while, in the act of blessing them, He was parted from them and taken up into glory. Then was sung that beautiful song, *Lift up your heads, O ye gates, and be ye lift up, ye everlasting doors, and the King of glory shall come in* (Psalm 24:7). But, my dear brethren, what does my telling you about Christ being gone into heaven matter, there *to appear in the presence of God for us* (Hebrews 9:24), unless you feel these things in your hearts and *set your affections on things above* (Colossians 3:2)?

The Greatest Sin

To reject Christ is the greatest sin you can commit, and the only one that seals your damnation.

Personal Interest in Atonement

Never think of the atonement of Christ without thinking that Christ's costly sacrifice was necessary for you. May God help us to think more of the sufferings of Christ, and may His love melt down our hearts.

Love – The Life of All Graces

Faith is a mere imagination unless it is proved by works. If we are believers, we have that faith that works by love and brings us near to God. If we have the grace of love to God in our hearts, we have every other grace. The grace of love is the life of all other graces.

Final Perseverance

You are setting out on a journey from a bad country, but never mind that. Take the staff of promise in your hand, and though you set out in weakness, you will be gloriously strengthened until you arrive at that *city which hath foundations, whose builder and maker is God* (Hebrews 11:10).

Repentance – The Last Companion

If I may be permitted to drop one tear as I enter the portals of the city of my God, it will be at taking an eternal leave of that beloved and profitable companion – repentance.

Duties Reciprocal

If I want a good servant, I will try to improve his mind. I will teach him what is proper. I will try to be a good master, and then, I have no doubt that we will be very happy together. I wish it were well understood that all duties are to be reciprocal. Let there be good parents, and we will have good children. Let there be good employers, and we will have good employees.

Let there be good tradesmen, and we will have good customers. Let us do as we should, and all will be well. These are very plain observations, but they are often necessary.

Promises – The Saint's Weapons

Nothing in the world repels the enemy's temptations so well as when we can fasten on a good promise from God's Word and set it in opposition to the devil's malice against our precious souls.

Fit for Heaven

If an unholy man were to get into heaven, he would feel like a hog in a flower garden.

Pride – Worldly

A rich man would be ashamed of himself if a poor beggar boy would claim such a relationship as the lowliest Christian may claim to God. Oh, what a mercy it is to be enabled to say, *Our Father which art in heaven* (Matthew 6:9)!

Wisdom – Heavenly

Heavenly wisdom creates heavenly utterance. There is something in preaching the gospel with the Holy Spirit sent down from heaven that I long to get at. If we deal with divine realities, we should feel them as such, and then the people will in general feel with us and will acknowledge the power that does wonders on the heart. Dry, formal discussion-type preaching leaves the hearers just where it found them.

Preaching to the End

If all the physicians in the world were to tell me that I must renounce my ministry on account of my increasing weakness, and that such weakness would increase until a speedy death would be the result, I would keep my fee in my pocket and would labor until I die.

True Religion

True religion is doctrinal, experimental, and practical. If we possessed only doctrinal religion, it would lead to Antinomianism; if only experimental, to enthusiasm; if only practical, to pharisaism. Therefore, if we want to be partakers of the religion of Jesus, all three must be united; we must not separate them.

Prayer

A prayerless soul is a Christless soul, and a Christless soul is a hopeless soul.

Noisy Preaching

Speaking of the loud sermons of those preachers who confuse noise with power, he said, "These sermons, sir, remind me of a hailstorm upon clay roofing tiles. They make a great deal of noise, but produce no impression."

Love of Preaching

I would rather be shut up in my coffin than shut out of the pulpit. As old, as very old, as I am, yet still I trust I find it not less my privilege than my duty to dedicate the very last of my declining strength to His glory in the accomplishment of the sacred work. If a physician would tell me that my life is in danger if I continue to preach, I will answer him, *Neither count I my life dear unto myself, so that I may finish my course with joy, and the ministry which I have received of the Lord Jesus, to testify the gospel of the grace of God* (Acts 20:24). So said Paul, and so says poor old Rowland Hill.

Love and Humility

If you want to see the height of the hill of God's eternal love, you must go down into the valley of humility.

The Purpose of Preaching

It is a thousand times better to have the simplicity of Peter than the eloquence of an orator if we are to be made useful to the souls of our fellow creatures! That preaching is always best that best answers the purpose of preaching.

Conversions – The Miracles of the Ministry

Some people may have concerns that little can be done because miracles are lacking and the gift of tongues is withdrawn. Undoubtedly, Peter had a notable proof at hand of the doctrine he preached when the lame man, who just before had been healed by the name of the Lord Jesus, was leaping in the temple (Acts 3). However, miracles never cease while souls are converted to God, nor will tongues ever be lacking while the wonderful change brought about by the grace of God so loudly proclaims the praises of His wonder-working power. Let heathens see what grace can do on a real convert, and we do not need to be discouraged any longer for lack of miracles and tongues.

Dissenters by Birth

I remember once having a conversation with a man, and I asked him whether there were any good people in the town in which he lived. He replied, "We were all born Dissenters."

I said to him, "Do not tell me about those who were born Dissenters, but of Dissenters who were born again."

Shifting Parsons

Doors that were opened by incredible effort and hard work are now, in many places, almost entirely shut. You must know that the modern branches of conceited divinity, after they have done all the mischief in their power, up they fly, like balloons, and fall down again, after their inflammable air is a little evaporated, to do the same mischief elsewhere, wherever the judgment of God allows them to fall. I am determined to let the doors be shut rather than to employ the young chaplains of old Beelzebub in the sacred work of God.

A Minister's Coat of Arms

We need ministers with the zeal of Luther and the quiet, patient spirit of a Moravian missionary – men who are willing to adopt the cross for their coat of arms, a heart above the world for their crest, and to adopt *spend and be spent* (2 Corinthians 12:15) as their motto.

Ministerial Training

However high the attainments of a preacher may be, it is the *furnace of affliction* alone (Isaiah 48:10) that will enable him, from deep sympathy of spirit, to *weep with those who weep* (Romans 12:10), and to fully administer to the *bruised reed*

(Isaiah 42:3; Matthew 12:20) the rich supports of the gospel of grace.

Reproof without Offense

After dining with a group of ministers and friends, he said to his servant, in the hearing of a member of the group who had drunk too freely, "Charles, when you see a minister drunk, don't talk about it, for you will harm the cause of Christ; but whenever you see me drunk, tell all the world about it."

Help the Poor

Those who have it in their power should make the poor man's pocket the bank of their riches.

Missionaries

Describing the sort of men who were needed for the mission field, he said, "We want men with good, plain sense in their heads and plenty of grace in their hearts – men who can make a good wheelbarrow and talk to the inquisitive heathen about the love of Christ the whole time they are putting it together."

State Church

Speaking of the Established Church, Mr. Hill remarked, "While Christianity was supported by her native purity, her beauties were all her own, and the dignity of her power on the hearts of millions had a glorious effect. But when the Church was embraced by the State and began to partake of the riches of the world, she partook of its corruptions also. When it became respectable to make a profession of Christianity, outward Christians, without inward Christianity, made their appearance in abundance. No wonder, therefore, that as Christianity rolled on through the muddy channel of worldly applause and courtly approbation, it became deeply contaminated thereby."

Waiting to Be Gracious

Allow me to conclude by pleading with you, by all that is dear and tender, to lay these things most closely to heart. While I thus address you, I feel the most affectionate sympathy toward you that words can possibly express. I urge you, therefore, to go home and take this message to heart. The expanded arms of a dear Redeemer are now open to embrace every returning prodigal that is enabled to receive this gospel call. None are too wicked for mercy to receive. The Lord of love has given you the promise, "Whosoever comes to Me, *I will in no wise cast out*" (John 6:37). *Even so, come, Lord Jesus* (Revelation 22:20). Amen and Amen!

The following hymn, composed by Mr. Hill for the comfort of a dying member of his church, will provide an appropriate conclusion to these fragments of his ministry:

The Prayer of the Dying Christian

Gently, my Savior, let me down
To slumber in the arms of death:
I rest my soul on Thee alone,
E'en till my last expiring breath.

Soon will the storm of life be o'er,
And I shall enter endless rest:
There shall I live to sin no more,

And bless Thy name, forever blest.

Dear Savior, let Thy will be done;
Like yielding clay I humbly lie.
May every murmuring thought be gone,
Most peacefully resign'd to die.

Bid me possess sweet peace within,
Let childlike patience keep my heart;
Then shall I feel my heaven begin
Before my spirit hence depart.

Yes, and a brighter heaven still
Awaits my soul through His rich grace,
Who shall His word of truth reveal,
Till called to sing His endless praise.

Hasten Thy chariot, God of love,
And take me from this world of woe;
I long to reach those joys above,
And bid farewell to all below.

There shall my raptured spirit raise
Still louder notes than angels sing;
High glories to Emmanuel's grace,
My God, my Savior, and my King.

Part 4

Sermons, etc.

Chapter 8

Christ Crucified, the Sum and Substance of the Scriptures

The following sermon, entitled "Christ Crucified, the Sum and Substance of the Scriptures," was preached by Rowland Hill on June 8, 1783, at the opening of Surrey Chapel, and it provides a good example of his usual style of preaching.

> *But we preach Christ crucified, unto the Jews a stumblingblock, and unto the Greeks foolishness; but unto them which are called, both Jews and Greeks, Christ the power of God, and the wisdom of God.* (1 Corinthians 1:23-24)

Through the abundant mercy and providence of a gracious God, we enter today upon public worship in this place. May it prove to be the beginning of happy days to thousands who are already born of God, and the cause of future joy to tens of thousands who are now dead in trespasses and sins!

I take it for granted that the majority of my congregation believes in the immortality of the soul and that the Bible is our only guide to a blessed eternity. How great the responsibility is to care for immortal souls! Well might an apostle cry out, *Who is sufficient for these things?* (2 Corinthians 2:16).

It is good for us that it is written, *Our sufficiency is of God* (2 Corinthians 3:5), and while I undertake this solemn work with a trembling heart, I thank God for the promise given: *As thy day, so shall thy strength be* (Deuteronomy 33:25).

The subject chosen will direct me to consider the substance of those leading doctrines of the gospel that I intend to preach among you. Christ crucified may be said to be the Alpha and Omega of all the Bible. There is not a promise given that does not refer to Him. There is not a warning or judgment pronounced where He is not represented as a shelter from the storm and a refuge for the guilty. Not a prophecy is revealed in which the testimony of Jesus is not the spirit of prophecy. Not one priestly institution was ever ordained, not one bleeding bullock or slaughtered lamb ever stained a Jewish altar, except what was meant to represent a crucified Redeemer as the Lamb of God, *slain from the foundation of the world* (Revelation 13:8).

All the lives of the patriarchs, filled with unusual and instructive providences, demonstrate the fullness of God's grace. While we pleasingly read of the tenderness of a forgiving Joseph to his returning brethren, the meekness of a Moses, the strength of a Samson, the patience of a Job, and the wisdom of a Solomon, at once we see all their excellent qualities as faint representations of Him in whom dwells *all the fullness of the Godhead bodily* (Colossians 2:9); of Him who stands as the Creator of each inferior star while shining forth with His own innate glories as the Sun of righteousness (Malachi 4:2). He appears as the only light in a dark world. Without this light, how great would our darkness be!

Do we need any stronger proof than what is given in the first two chapters of this epistle? Read them when you have time, and see with what force of reasoning the apostle dwells upon the subject, proving that the very *wisdom of this world is foolishness with God* (1 Corinthians 3:19), and that it is impossible for the mere carnal or unenlightened mind to comprehend the glories of the spiritual world, for *the natural man receiveth not the things of the Spirit of God: for they are foolishness unto him: neither can he know them; because they are spiritually discerned* (1 Corinthians 2:14).

However, if someone thinks that even more evidence is necessary, let the history of the heathen world in general be brought as a confirmation of the need and blessing of revelation, wherein all the wisdom of the wise regarding the knowledge of God is proved to be absolute foolishness. Consider the foolishness that disgraces the system of the wisest philosophers when they lack this revelation! All the learning of Rome and Greece did not prevent them from adding preposterous and detestable deities to their darkened and vain and foolish imaginations (Romans 1:21).

While every vile lust and monstrous abomination was even deified for their adoration, there was hardly an idea to be found among them of a God with those infinite perfections that the Bible reveals. If this was the condition of the more educated and civilized part of mankind, it is no wonder that we find the rest of the fallen race, if possible, still more deeply immersed in this universal ignorance of God.

The unhappy sailor who is tossed about in the midst of the ocean without either chart or compass, and who is made the sport of every variable wind, cannot represent to us a deeper scene of misery and distress than we would sustain if we were deprived of this blessed Book. The Bible alone proclaims a God of infinite purity and eternal justice who is endued with all possible perfections. May we not, therefore, conclude that the Bible is the most invaluable blessing that God ever gave to man? Will it not, therefore, be my highest honor and greatest glory to recommend this Book to you as the main object of your studies and delight, and to adopt it for myself as the only guide of all my public duties in this place?

However, no matter how much these sacred records proclaim their own authenticity and authority, it is well known that there is a certain type of people who are immersed in idleness and self-indulgence, and who are consequently by no means worthy to be classed among the most thinking and educated of the day. These people, for lack of real argument, are glad to use the weapons of mocking and ridicule against the blessings of revelation.

It is a matter of consolation to the serious mind that God has not left Himself without witness respecting the authenticity of His own Book. The fulfilment of prophecy in particular is the great external argument that leaves the world without excuse. What person of an honest mind can read some late admirable dissertations upon this subject by Bishop Newton[13] and others without having his mind at once filled with wonder and astonishment, and cleansed from every hint of unbelief?

I am not at all ashamed to stand up for the internal evidences of Christianity, nor will the accusation of fanaticism deter me from giving my testimony to a truth so profitable to mankind and so perfectly consistent with the nature of the pure and holy God. Was there ever a system formed or thought of by man that promised the incredible blessing of a change of mind – a change that transforms every sinful tendency of the soul *from darkness to light, and from the power of Satan unto God* (Acts 26:18)? Yet the Bible abounds with promises of this sort.

What else can be the meaning of these various phrases found in the Bible, such as the circumcision of the heart, a new heart, a heart of stone exchanged for a heart of flesh, a new creation, a new nature, a divine nature, a spiritual mind, a new birth,

---

[13] Bishop Thomas Newton (1704-1782) of the Church of England wrote a book, published in 1754, entitled *Dissertations on the Prophecies, Which Have Remarkably Been Fulfilled, and at This Time Are Fulfilling in the World.*

putting on the Lord Jesus, abiding in Him, dwelling in Him, being one with Him, etc.? What can be the meaning of all these various phrases unless they are interpreted as God's gracious plan of putting His own pure and Holy Spirit into the sinner's heart as a glorious living power to lift him up above the world and to enable him by his outward actions, while here below, to *adorn the doctrine of God our Savior in all things* (Titus 2:10)? I am confident, therefore, to conclude that these are promises that only God could truly give, since no one except God could possibly fulfil them. May those who believe them prove their fulfilment by living to His glory!

In vain, therefore, do the simpletons of the day use their meager powers to try to pick away at the supposed absurdities of some of the miracles, or some imagined mistakes in chronology, while such significant proof can be produced that the book we preach from is the Book of God.

Nor should they be so unreasonable as to expect others to be unbelievers while it remains a matter of doubt whether they are unbelievers themselves. The integrity of the profession of far too many of them must be doubted while the sinfulness and self-indulgence of their lives, and the wickedness of their behavior, give the world all possible reason to conclude that when they say they *do not* believe, they mean they *dare not* believe.

An ignorant and depraved deist is a character, of all others, the most contemptible. Imagine someone who is a novice in learning laughing at Julius Caesar's commentaries on the Gallic and Civil Wars, refusing to allow his noble understanding to be duped by such idle tales and pitying the gullible multitudes who are so infatuated as to believe them. Equally insignificant is that person's character who laughs at a book, the authenticity of which he never examined, while those who have found rational learning to be an excellent handmaid to religion believe that no stronger proof can be brought for the authenticity of the commentaries of Julius Caesar than has already been produced for the Word of God.

But enough of this. Christ crucified is the subject of the Bible, and we have determined that this Bible is the Word of God. I have already hinted that this is the only subject that I intend to deal with among you. What is to be understood by preaching Christ crucified? First, concerning the person of Christ, and in this I am most firmly persuaded respecting His divine nature, He is the everlasting Jehovah, Creator of all things, God over all, blessed for evermore.

I understand this to be as plainly revealed as the existence of God. First, all the powers of creation are ascribed to Him, but the brightest among angels cannot create an atom, or give existence to a worm. As creatures, they are nothing in themselves, for in God they live, and move, and have their being (Acts 17:28). Our God and Savior the Lord Jesus was not such a being as that. He was the Creator of all things, and consequently the Creator of angels. John says, *All things were made by Him, and without Him was not any thing made that was made. In Him was life* (John 1:3-4).

The author of Hebrews adds his testimony to that of John, for unto the Son he affirms that it is said:

> *Thy throne, O God, is for ever and ever: a sceptre of righteousness is the sceptre of Thy kingdom. Thou hast loved righteousness, and hated iniquity; therefore God, even Thy God, hath anointed Thee with the oil of gladness above Thy fellows. And Thou, Lord, in the beginning hast laid the foundation of the earth, and the heavens are the works of Thine hands: they shall perish; but Thou remainest; and they all shall wax old as doth a garment; and as a vesture shalt Thou fold them up, and they shall be*

changed: but Thou art the same, and Thy years shall not fail. (Hebrews 1:8-12)

So that some, after all this, would not ignorantly mistake Jesus for the framer of the building, by the superior orders of God His Father, and not the actual Lord and possessor of the building itself, the apostle Paul guards this sacred truth and assures us that not only by Him, but for Him were all things created (Colossians 1:16). All worlds were made by His great decree, and they are upheld by Him as their eternal Lord. All their vast inhabitants, from the lowest reptile to the highest angel, are the workmanship of His hands, and still exist by His Almighty care. Thrones, dominions, principalities, and powers were brought into existence by Him and for Him, and by His eternal providence they still exist to manifest His infinite praise.

It is well known that objections in abundance have been invented to invalidate the strongest arguments upon this subject. However, it is undoubtedly clear that from the plain reading of the Scriptures, the greater part of mankind by far have been led to worship Christ as God. Consequently, if Christ is not God, then the Bible itself has led thousands to a wrong object of supreme adoration.

This, however, is not the time to enter more fully into the controversy, so I will give the following observations as outlines for further improvement. Which of the names, titles, or attributes of the great eternal God are not given to our God and Savior also? Is God the Father called Jehovah? So is God the Son. Is God the Father called the great God and the only wise God? So is God the Son. Is God the Father the Lord of Hosts? So is God the Son. Is God the Father the Author and Giver of life? So is God the Son, who *quickeneth whom He will* (John 5:21). Is God the Father the Almighty, the mighty God, and the everlasting Father? So is God the Son (Isaiah 9:6). Is

God the Father the Searcher of hearts? So is God the Son. Does God the Father receive the honor of prayer and praise from His creatures? So does God the Son, who never gave a single reproof to those who brought it, although we repeatedly find that He was worshipped by men below, as well as adored by angels above. Are these not sufficient arguments to demonstrate this everlasting truth? Does this not prove Him to be the *express image* of His Father's person (Hebrews 1:3)? If He were lacking in even a single attribute, how could He be His Father's express image?

Therefore, my beloved brethren, we will glory in the Godhead of our Savior, and will gladly lay it as the grand foundation stone of the gospel upon which our superstructure is built. We will make this place to resound with the honors due to His eternal and ever-blessed name – *King of kings, and Lord of lords* (1 Timothy 6:15; Revelation 19:16).

The next observation that occurs regarding the person of Christ is that just as we believe Him to be the eternal God, so by taking our nature upon Him, we believe Him to be very man. This is the great mystery of godliness, *God was manifest in the flesh* (1 Timothy 3:16). That God might be just, and yet the justifier of those who believe (Romans 3:26), He prepared a body for His well-beloved Son. Jesus fulfilled His Father's will in that body; as man He appears for men. He magnifies the law and makes it honorable by bringing in an everlasting righteousness on the sinner's behalf. This truth has not been any less opposed in ancient times[14] than the truth of His divinity is opposed in the present day. All who are acquainted with the history of the earlier ages of the church know with what fervor the error was promoted that Christ, whatever He might be in appearance, was not really man. However, the error largely died with its promoters, so we pass it by and move on to consider the

---

14   This was the error of the numerous sects of the Manichees.

situation of mankind that made it necessary for such a Savior to undertake the recovery of our fallen race.

I not only dwell upon this as a necessary introduction to the glories of the recovery of man, but also so you may know what I firmly believe respecting this unpleasant truth of the fall of man. Man was created in a state of the most complete purity. He was the delight of his Creator while he continued in that happy state. He soon fell and became immediately repulsive to his God. Sin is infinitely loathsome to the divine nature, and so the creature whom He made was no longer the object of His delight. All real good was instantly withdrawn. No principle of holiness any longer abided in him. He was given over to the will of the adversary and was led captive by the Enemy who first tempted him to rebel, who works upon his unruly passions, and who completely mars every quality of the soul.

Being thus fallen, it is no surprise that it necessarily follows that the imaginations of his heart are only evil, and that continually (Genesis 6:5). How notably does universal experience prove this dreadful fact! Are we dreaming when we say that a generation is found that denies the fall? Can they be serious? What is to be believed if the fall is to be denied? As believers of revelation, I first address this group of people.

We examine, for a little while, God's characterization of man – and God knows man better than man knows himself. God declares, *There is not a just man upon earth that doeth good and sinneth not* (Ecclesiastes 7:20). He declares that *the heart is deceitful above all things, and desperately wicked* (Jeremiah 17:9), and that, consequently, no one living can be justified in His sight by his works (Romans 3:20). God says, *If we say that we have no sin, we deceive ourselves, and the truth is not in us* (1 John 1:8), and *If we say we have not sinned, we make Him a liar* (1 John 1:10). He says that we are born in sin, conceived in sin (Psalm 51:5), dead in sin (Ephesians 2:5), and sold under sin (Romans 7:14). God's Word tells us that evil is present with us (Romans 7:21), that in us dwelleth no good thing (Romans 7:18), that all are *gone out of the way*, that all are *become unprofitable*, and that *there is none that doeth good, no not one* (Romans 3:12). We are told that there is *none to uphold* (Isaiah 63:5), that every mouth must be stopped, and that all the world, both Jews and Gentiles, are *become guilty before God* (Romans 3:19).

But why do I need to provide more evidence? If I were to go over half the Bible, either directly or indirectly, we would see some evidence of the fall that we had not noticed before. Which of the purest characters of Scripture was not defiled by sin? What did those rivers of blood under the Jewish dispensation mean except as typical representations to the children of God, in those ages of the church, of their daily need of atonement for their innumerable sins, both known and unknown. An atonement was ordered for sins of ignorance committed against a God of infinite purity, who demanded an atonement of infinite satisfaction. What does that incessant voice of prayer mean that is mourning over the evil and punishment of sin that we find arising from every lip acquainted with God? Why do we find such dreadful histories throughout the Scriptures, as rolls written within and without, with weeping, lamentation, and woe, unless man was a sinner before God?

Again, let the history of the world in general be called to bear witness against itself. The contents of the record of every nation under heaven is simply an alternate history of misery and oppression. What rivers of innocent blood have been shed to please the pride of tyrants! Meanwhile, their poor deluded supporters, forgetting to serve that God in righteousness and true holiness who fills His throne above, have commanded the miserable slaves to obey the horrid mandates of these gods below, these dreadful monsters in human shape.

The millions of suffering infants will next produce their testimony to the truth, who, though never having actually transgressed the laws of God, suffer in this world for their original guilt, and though we trust we have sufficient grounds from Scripture to believe that these are their only sufferings, yet I am sure that their sufferings in this world sufficiently prove them to be sinners from the womb. All the groans of universal nature bring up the dreadful rear of punishments due to the sin of man from a just and holy God.

The observation of the apostle Paul does not need any proof or comment, which declares that *the whole creation groaneth and travaileth in pain together* (Romans 8:22) until God will put away sin by destroying its very being from the earth.

This was the situation of ruined man when God the Savior came to redeem. He comes in His body, prepared for Him by almighty love. He stands as the Mediator, bearing in His own person all that was due to mankind from the justice of God. He fulfils those ancient prophecies recorded of Him, for the Messiah was cut off (Daniel 9:26) – not for Himself, but for His people. Thereby He finished the transgression, made an end of sin, made reconciliation for iniquity, and brought in everlasting righteousness on the sinner's behalf. Thus, by the sacrifice of Himself once offered, while He dies upon the cross, He calls the sinner to live, revealing Himself as *the Lamb of God, that taketh away the sins of the world* (John 1:29).

Respecting this glorious work of redemption, with His dying lips He tells us, *It is finished* (John 19:30), while by His repeated word of promise we are invited to place all our hopes upon Him for grace in time, and for glory in eternity.

In this blessed name alone, my beloved brethren, I preach salvation among you. He only must be exalted by me as your all in all. If I would dare to preach to you in any other name, or point you to any other hope, avoid me as your enemy. You are ignorant indeed if you do not know that you are sinners before God. You are breakers of the law, and I do not, I dare not, point you to that law against which you have so repeatedly transgressed. Therefore, withdraw every shadow of confidence that you may have on account of anything you have done or can do as the terms of your acceptance. God is of purer eyes than to behold iniquity (Habakkuk 1:13). You cannot stand when He appears (Malachi 3:2), for how *can man be justified with God? or how can he be clean that is born of a woman?* (Job 25:4).

It is Jesus who has *put away sin by the sacrifice of Himself* (Hebrews 9:26). If you view Christ crucified as the object of your faith, and if you make Him the only plea for your acceptance before God, you do not need to fear the penalties of the curse. Never was justice so magnified before, nor mercy so conspicuously revealed. If the great Creator had delivered up a thousand angels, that would not have been a sacrifice anywhere close to equaling that of God not even sparing His well-beloved Son (Romans 8:32) when He stood as man for men to bear the vengeance of God's wrath.

Oh, the justice that demanded such an atonement! Oh, the mercy that revealed such a salvation for a ruined world! Can sinners hear of such mercy and resist it – sinners who are doomed to die for sins greater in number than the sands on the seashore? Oh, how hard those hearts must be that can be evidence against such astonishing love and refuse to yield themselves to Him who paid so great a price for sinners so worthless and so vile! By the love of God, I plead with you who have never yet been captivated by such grace to no longer delay, but to hasten to be the firstfruits unto the Lord this day in this place. The most sinful are welcome. May God help you to come.

Thus, agreeably to the language of our text, Christ crucified appears to be the substance of all that the gospel reveals for the salvation of mankind. Are all Christians to begin as the followers of a humble, crucified Redeemer? Are we to glory in nothing else *save in the cross of our Lord Jesus Christ*, by whom the world is crucified unto them, and they unto the world (Galatians 6:14)? Then what manner of people we should be in all conversation and godliness (2 Peter 3:11), since being bought with a price we cease to be our own (1 Corinthians 6:19-20), but are bound by the strongest obligations to glorify God in our bodies and spirits, which are His!

Not only do we adore our Savior as our dying Lord, but also as our risen Conqueror over all our foes. In that, it appears that the victory is complete. All our enemies are now subdued by Him who has *led captivity captive* (Ephesians 4:8) and lives to triumph over them all (Colossians 2:15). He will swallow up death in victory (1 Corinthians 15:54), and the very existence of sin will soon be no more.

Being thus exalted at the right hand of the Majesty on high (Acts 2:33; Hebrews 1:3) as God, He cannot change like the sons of men do, for with Him is no variableness nor shadow of turning (James 1:17), being the same yesterday, today, and forever (Hebrews 13:8). He rests in God's love. Therefore, having loved His own, He must love them to the end (John 13:1). It is impossible that His intercession for His people can be ineffective. We know that the Father always hears Him (John 11:42), and that by this the Father is glorified in the Son, and the Son in Him (John 17:1).

Oh, the inexpressible blessing of having such an Advocate with the Father to plead our cause before the eternal throne (1 John 2:1)! Why should guilt ever again keep us from drawing near to God while the sinner's Friend must be heard, whose plea must assuredly prevail? Sheltered from the penalties of a broken law, all that is due to sin is done away as though it had never been. We are protected by that arm that is *mighty to save* (Isaiah 63:1), and the power of sin will not be permitted any longer to prevail. Yes, we must and shall be holy while the grand design of this salvation must assuredly be brought to pass. The death of Christ is the death of sin, and it is the great procuring cause of holiness to the world, for He came to *purify unto Himself a peculiar people, zealous of good works* (Titus 2:14).

How, then, do some among you say that the doctrines of grace tend to make us careless in the rules of our obedience, or that from them may be advanced that detested principle, *Let us do evil that good may come* (Romans 3:8)? And how is it that these inconsistent objectors (we are sure that they are false witnesses) against that cause which, with a humble confidence, we are bold to maintain as the cause of Christ, how is it that with the same breath they can scoff at the strictness of our morals, and yet, as setters forth of strange doctrines (Acts 17:18), represent us as enemies to morality?

But are they really serious when they make the accusation, or do they mean it as something to terrify the ignorant? I will not further debate this with those who seem to be ignorant of what they say or what they claim, but I will only publicly declare that I suspect their honesty in the cheap accusation. Therefore, I am not so vain as to suppose that those who are predetermined to believe evil in opposition to all that can be said against it can be profited by my arguments, but rather, for the sake of recording my thoughts among you this day, I repeat the old stale objection, *Shall we continue in sin, that grace may abound?* (Romans 6:1). I answer, *God forbid* (Romans 6:2).

The doctrines of grace provide just the opposite of what our enemies would represent. My text directs me to prove the point. Christ crucified is the wisdom of God, and is the power of God to all who believe (1 Corinthians 1:23-24). The knowledge of Christ crucified will and must lead us into those paths of divine obedience by which *wisdom is justified of all her children* (Luke 7:35). By our consistent and upright behavior in every social and meaningful situation in life, the world may be constrained to cry, *What hath God wrought!* (Numbers 23:23).

Oh, the glorious consequences of this blessed salvation! How exclusive to itself is that power that is called *the power of God unto salvation to every one that believeth* (Romans 1:16). The Holy Spirit takes up the office of the sanctifier of the people of God. We are called today to honor His sanctifying influences, and as all the life and influence of holiness in this world depends upon His power, it cannot be said that a complete summary of the gospel has been delivered unless some notice is taken of this blessed truth.

Now *the high and lofty One that inhabiteth eternity* (Isaiah 57:15) lowers Himself to make the humbled sinner's heart the place of His gracious abode. Now, in a way of justice through the salvation brought about by the Son, God can impart His blessed Spirit to the heart of man. His holy nature takes up His residence within us, converting every inclination of the soul and enabling us to choose Him as our portion (Psalm 119:57; Lamentations 3:24). As a result of that happy choice, we love to follow the ways of His commandments with a special joy – yes, even *with joy unspeakable and full of glory* (1 Peter 1:8). Obedience is our heaven, and sin is the only hell we know below.

You who were once *dead in trespasses and sins* (Ephesians 2:1), who thought of nothing but those ways that lead to death, you know that the Redeemer has bought you by His blood and has worked that change upon your hearts by the living law of His grace within, which constrains all your sins to fall before you, just as Dagon fell before the ark (1 Samuel 5:3-4). While, like the worshippers of Baal of old who were humbled under a sense of their idolatry, you cast away your idols and cry, *The* LORD, *He is the God; the* LORD, *He is the God* (1 Kings 18:39). Do you therefore any longer need tedious lectures from the wearisome moralist to tell you to do good? Will it not rather seem that since you have been so gloriously changed by the power of God, and you find such freedom and delight in the ways of holiness, that you need a bridle rather than a spur? It is with the liberty of sons, not with the bondage of slaves, that you are taught to obey (Galatians 4:1-7).

You highly favored servants of the living God, come forth and bear your united testimonies with me to what you have felt and tasted of this glorious truth. Tell me, did you love holiness, or did you even know what holiness meant, until you knew the gospel and loved the Savior? Do you not yearn to be holy as God is holy (1 Peter 1:16)? O blessed longings, the longings that angels have, the desires that will result in a state completely as glorious as angels enjoy!

Go forth, therefore, my beloved brethren, and live for God. *Arise, shine, for your light is come, and the glory of the* Lord *is risen upon you* (Isaiah 60:1). Let it now be known that you love Jesus too much to offend Him, and that those sacred cords that bind angels to obey have been wrapped around your hearts and have made you the willing captives of this most pleasant grace, for the love of Christ constrains you (2 Corinthians 5:14).

Through the influences of the Holy Spirit, sin, that dwells in you (Romans 7:17), is now no longer your delight. Holiness is the object of your choice. The power of omnipotent grace must and will prevail, teaching you to abhor that which is evil and to cling to that which is good (Romans 12:9).

I think I hear you say, "We detest the horrid idea of being saved by a gospel that invalidates obedience to the law, for we love the gospel. It is God's great method of revealing a power to the heart by which we obey the law. Most gladly, therefore, do we welcome it as the rule of our life, and declare ourselves under its eternal dominion. Since the law is not made void, but is established by the gospel, we conclude that it must be as holy and eternal as God Himself, binding every creature capable of obeying under its immense demands.

"We judge, therefore, that God can sooner cease to be than to allow the least failure in the least decree. Nor can any time change Him who is unchangeable in His demands, or erase transgression from His eternal mind, or cause Him to do away with that law that is as holy and eternal as Himself. Therefore, we detest the idea of a milder law than that which He delivered to our first parents of old, and afterward confirmed on Mount Sinai to His Israel, lest we should say that a God of infinite perfections can, contrary to His own unchangeable nature, even permit or justify a law that allows imperfections in His creatures.

"Nor dare we acknowledge that strange idea, no matter how popular it is, of the holy God being won by what some believe to be the terms and conditions of our salvation, consisting of faith, repentance, sincere obedience, or whatever else (for these conditions are as various as those who propose them), lest we should be found to be advancing a doctrine that is derogatory to the holiness of God – for all acknowledge that this sincere obedience is imperfect at best. If it is imperfect, it is therefore sinful. We then cannot affirm that the infinitely pure and holy God can be pleased with that which has in it the nature of sin, and we believe that our arguments are abundantly strengthened by what we read in the Scriptures, of no other name being given whereby salvation is obtained (Acts 4:12). And while we further read that in man dwells no good thing (Romans 7:18), and that without Christ we can do nothing (John 15:5), we are apt to conclude that all these supposed conditions vanish like smoke; and we are so vain as to think we can prove that the philosophy of the doctrine is bad, and the divinity of it is a thousand times worse."

Thus have I been attempting somewhat to discuss the main doctrines of the gospel, which I intend to make the subject of my ministry in this place. No matter how much these blessed truths may appear to be foolishness to the world, yet to those whom Christ has chosen out of the world, they will appear to be the wisdom of God and the power of God unto their eternal salvation. May many be deeply convinced of the evil of sin and be constrained to run to our God and Savior Jesus, trusting in His righteousness alone for pardon and acceptance, and receiving the blessed influence of His Spirit so that they may be made *meet to be partakers of the inheritance of the saints in light* (Colossians 1:12).

Allow me to conclude with a word of application on the whole subject. You servants of the living God, I implore you to speak His praise by devoting yourselves to His glory so that the blaspheming world may be brought to shame by beholding your good conduct and conversation in Christ. Pay attention to your actions. *Whether therefore you eat, or drink, or whatsoever you do, do all to the glory of God* (1 Corinthians 10:31). I ask you also to be careful in regard to your temperament. In malice, be children (1 Corinthians 14:20). Parents, observe your children and let them teach you to forgive. Although they may be angry one minute, they forgive and love the next. There is nothing more worthy to be instilled than a holy temperament. *Learn of me*, says our Lord and Master, who was the pattern of meekness, *and you shall find rest unto your souls* (Matthew 11:29).

Lastly, by the love of God, let me ask you who are living in sin to consider this before it is too late. *Now is the accepted time; behold, now is the day of salvation* (2 Corinthians 6:2). The arms of tender mercy are open to receive you. Do not imagine that you lose your pleasures when you lose your sins, and that living to God will be a burdensome task. No, but thanks to God, thousands can declare that they never knew what it was to be redeemed from misery until they were redeemed from sin.

My whole soul prays that God would make you of that happy number. May this be so, Lord Jesus. Amen.

Chapter 9

The Objective of the Christian Ministry

We add the following prayer and sermon, delivered within a year of his death, at the age of eighty-nine; and although the style of the discourse is wandering, we consider it no ordinary production when we consider the preacher's age. Few who survive the allotted term of human life would be capable of such an effort. The mere sight of the old man in the pulpit speaking so sweetly of the truths of the gospel must have been a means of grace in itself. As the mind pictures the scene as you read this discourse, the power with which it was delivered seems transferred to the printed page. It undoubtedly lacks the strength and energy of his earlier sermons, but it is a sweet memorial of a gracious ministry.

A Prayer before the Sermon, April 29, 1832

O Lord, we give ourselves up to You. What a blessed thing it is to be strengthened with all might by Your Spirit in the inner man – to have God in us, and with us, while we call on His glorious name! Oh, that we may be enabled to look through all the weakness of the body for that spiritual strength that comes from You. But Lord, my own mind needs to be prepared by You.

Lord, You must give utterance to the preacher. Otherwise, he will speak ineffectively, and he needs to be made the instrument of bringing precious souls to You. This can never be done by him, but only by You alone as you use him, with the power originating from above. Lord, the people are before You. How can I get into their hearts? What can I say to them that will so deeply take root as to have a divine effect? You promise that Your gospel, which is at all times the same, will be in all ages of the church the power of God to the salvation of the soul.

We now most humbly pray that this may be the time of salvation to some sinners. How often do we grieve, O Lord, to see many people come to Your house on the Lord's Day who approve Your ordinances, yet neglect them! Is it not proof that their hearts are still not with You? Good God, when will the work be more profitably accomplished, and sinners be brought with all the powers of the gospel to give themselves up to You in deed and in truth?

Oh, that the Lord God would now give us all grace and cause us to solemnly surrender ourselves to Him as His right and His own – and let all who can be His. Oh, for a spirit of dedication to God! Oh, for power in prayer! Oh, for the unction of the living Spirit to live in all societies powerfully and divinely, to be poured on Zion universally, and to be poured out on all Your churches in the world!

We bless You for what You have been doing in heathen lands. We pray that it may be done even more successfully. May the strong working of Your almighty power be gloriously exemplified in all Your churches! May we feel the power of Your Holy Spirit so blessedly within us that the power of holiness will universally prevail.

The Objective of the Christian Ministry

**A Sermon Preached at Surrey Chapel,
April 29, 1832**
By Rowland Hill

> *But none of these things move me, neither count I my life dear unto myself, so that I might finish my course with joy, and the ministry, which I have received of the Lord Jesus, to testify the gospel of the grace of God.* (Acts 20:24)

Many times when I have stood in this pulpit, I have thought that all I could do would be to read my text, and afterward be dependent upon a holy God for holy thoughts, trusting to His merciful guidance to direct me to speak truths that may be impressed on your mind so that the Spirit of holiness might be communicated to your souls in this way. It is a difficult matter for me now to even read my text, but blessed be God, my heart still echoes to the truth of these things – and there are no words that I have met with yet that sound like the words that echo from the house of God.

But I have been thinking. How can I, such an insignificant man, presume to address you in the language of such a great man as the apostle Paul, who preached the gospel with the Holy Spirit sent down from heaven with such warm and astonishing zeal, and who was as blessed as he was with a spirit like his Master's?

They say that when the young Grecians were training up to their work of death, the first work they had to do was to see how far they could shoot. Although the target was placed beyond their reach, they aimed at it as though they could reach it, for they believed that the day was coming when their strength would be sufficient to enable them to send the arrow home. O

God, help us never to be afraid of Your high commands because we poor feeble creatures cannot reach them. I am commanded to be a follower of God, and I am told in this invaluable Book that my God can do far more abundantly for me above all that I can ask or think (Ephesians 3:20). We should not form our desires according to human expectations, but according to the riches of the divine promises. Oh, glory be to His name! We have here that which eye has not seen, ear has not heard, nor has ever entered into the heart of man to comprehend (1 Corinthians 2:9)!

Paul is now about to leave the people of Ephesus. In this chapter, we are told that he sends for the elders of Ephesus to meet him at Miletus, a village that was probably close to the seashore. He was likely not permitted to go far up into the land since he was then a prisoner and was about to be taken as a prisoner to be tried and condemned to death at Rome. Here he takes his last, beautiful, final farewell of the people of Ephesus, where amid much contention he had been preaching to them the gospel of Christ. It was also where he had been establishing the glorious truths of the gospel of Christ in opposition to all the demented plans of the worshippers of the great goddess Diana of that city.

Lord, help me to preach the Word this morning, not only with some comfort to myself, but with some blessing to You. My dear brethren, you have need to pray more fervently now than ever, for I cannot preach as I used to preach, and therefore, since I cannot preach as I would desire, you should pray even more so that you do not miss the blessing of the message.

What is it that first presents itself to our consideration in these words? (We must simply go through it.) *Neither count I my life dear unto myself.* But it is very dear, nevertheless. I have a spark of immortality kindled within me, a life that God has secured for Himself by the purchase of His redeeming blood, and which He intends to make a habitation for Himself through His eternal Spirit. My life, then, is invaluable; why should I not then esteem it dear to me?

The apostle certainly means here that he was not at all afraid to sacrifice his present life for the sake of that future glory that he was to have bestowed upon him in the world to come. Oh, that we could live as we should live, and every moment live as unto God! Then we would see that a life of carnality, a life of worldly enjoyment, is a life of no meaning or importance to us.

What are the few hours that we spend here below when they are compared with that vast eternity that is before all of us – that eternity that I know I will soon begin, but who can tell when I will end it? Abel has now been lifting up his high praises to God for nearly six thousand years, and this morning he begins them all again. Although here on earth we get tired of singing the same song for lack of variety, there is something so new and glorious in the person and sufficiency of the Redeemer that it will always be a new song while we sing old ones. May the Lord prepare our hearts and put them in tune to sing His glorious praise forever! But let us go on.

So that I might finish my course with joy. Well, that is the thing – to finish with joy. We must first begin well. Oh, you young ones, are you beginning well? It is lovely to see the first stages of life most solemnly dedicated and devoted to God. We like to see the blossoms in the spring, but we like much better to see the fruit in the summer, and we like it best of all when it ripens in the autumn and when it answers the purpose for which its fertility was designed. So may the Lord grant that you may all begin well. Oh, that some prayers may now be offered up in your young minds that you may begin well, and begin today. If you have not yet begun this journey, begin now. May you continue better than you have so far. May you increase your strength in the Lord. May you end best of all, finishing your course with joy.

Neither count I my life dear unto myself, so that I may finish my course with joy. My dear brethren, this concerns all of you. Some of this Holy Book does not concern you all, but this does concern you all. God put you in the right path, and may the Lord grant that you will find your souls so sweetly accustomed to walk in this path that you may never step a single step aside.

Oh, when will this be sufficiently admired in the fullness of the command? *Be ye steadfast, unmovable, always abounding in the work of the Lord* (1 Corinthians 15:58). Keep to that always. Give yourselves no time except for God and His glory. You might say, "Sir, you don't know our lives. Our time is very much taken up. We have a business to run. We must take care of our families. We have much work to do while we are in this world." Very well. Work on. Only remember that in the midst of your labor, in the midst of your calling, whatever it may be, to keep the fear of God warm in your hearts and His love abiding in you so that while you are filling that sphere of life in which Providence has placed you, you may be filling it up to the glory of His dear name. Christian tradesmen are honorable characters, and I am sure that you may glorify God in your occupations more than many poor lazy creatures who have nothing to hinder them from being always active for God.

I have sometimes said that the world seems to me to be made up of a top and a bottom. It is froth at the top and mud at the bottom, and if there is any clear water, it is in the middle of society. If you are in that situation that you have all your time occupied, glory be to God. There is no lawful situation in which you cannot serve Him; otherwise, the apostle Paul would not have said, *Not slothful in business, fervent in spirit, serving the Lord* (Romans 12:11). Neither could the apostle have commanded that if anyone will not work, *neither should he eat* (2 Thessalonians 3:10).

Don't be concerned about your position, but fill it up for God. Remember that whatever capacity you are in, even in the smallest circumstance of life, you are directed to glorify God in the accomplishment of every duty. Whether you eat, or whether you drink, or whatsoever you do, you must do it all to the glory of God (1 Corinthians 10:31). You must have but one goal. Campbell was an excellent writer. He used to put at the conclusion of the treatises that he wrote, "Soli deo gloria" – "To God alone be all the glory." Let nothing be done but to the glory of God. All human actions, all worldly actions, may do as much to the glory of God as I may do by preaching to the glory of God. But let us see what else the apostle says.

None of these things move me, neither count I my life dear unto myself, so that I might finish my course with joy, and the ministry, which I have received of the Lord Jesus, to testify the gospel of the grace of God. Now this is our next business. May God keep us to it. The apostle in this short but very beautiful address to the elders of Ephesus has this beautiful expression: *Testifying both to the Jews, and also to the Greeks, repentance toward God and faith toward our Lord Jesus Christ* (Acts 20:21). What a comprehensive idea that is!

While I feel myself a sinner, let me live every moment as one who is repentant before Him, because I am a sinner. Then let the eye of faith be focused on the Lord Jesus Christ so that I may see Him in the splendor of His majesty and the richness of His grace as He pours down salvation upon my precious soul. Let me always know that He has done that great work for me that I never could have done for myself. Not only did He put away sin (that is the good news – the gospel) by the sacrifice of Himself upon the tree, and brought in everlasting righteousness whereby alone His church can be redeemed, but in mercy

He has established a divine power to be sent into the souls of His elect so that they may be sealed by receiving the promise of His Holy Spirit, the sealing of the Spirit of promise *until the day of redemption* (Ephesians 4:30).

However, I cannot see into the heavenly Book as fully as it lies open before the eyes of infinite knowledge. How, then, can I have any evidence that my name is written in the Lamb's Book of Life? The only evidence of that is by feeling it. Indeed, my brethren, the evidence is only by feeling His blessed image impressed upon our hearts. It is a very common custom among fine people who are fond of themselves to send their pictures to one another, but when you send a picture, the best picture or representation you can get is only a picture. You cannot send a speaking picture or a thinking picture to anyone. It is merely an inanimate representation.

But how gloriously does our blessed God work upon the heart when He puts His lovely image within us, when we as lively stones are built up as spiritual temples to the Lord (1 Peter 2:5), are created anew in Him, and have new life poured through every part of the soul. We know in whom we have believed (2 Timothy 1:12). These are the only evidences on which we can depend.

You never did, and I am very certain you never would, no matter how long I live, hear me preach any evidence that a man is right with God except by the implantation of His blessed image on the heart. I know that some people cry out, "Oh, I am sure I will be saved, for there is such and such a promise." Someone else says, "Oh, I am sure I am forgiven, for I have such liberty." However, these people are often depending on outward impressions.

Brethren, there is only one evidence that the heart is right with God and that it is right according to the Word of God: we love Him because we keep His commandments (John 14:15; 1 John 5:3). If the power of sin is mortified in me, if I have these abominable evils banished from my heart, and if I am enabled to put my foot on all my sinful lusts, then I am a conqueror, and more than a conqueror (Romans 8:37), through the strength of omnipotence reigning in my heart – the strength of Jesus Christ, my omnipotent God and Savior. When this is the case, I am sure it is right with me.

If you ever go near a person's house where there are a great number of noble and important visitors, you say, "Some great man lives here, or else he would not have such great company." Now, my dear brethren, it is true that God has promised to make your hearts the *habitation of God through the Spirit* (Ephesians 2:22). He cannot give a greater promise. He sends His spiritual graces down into our souls, and these are the graces that are my evidence that my heart is right with God. Then I feel the blessed image that He has created within my soul. This is in agreement with that fine expression of the apostle Paul, where he says, *We all, with open face beholding as in a glass the glory of the Lord* (2 Corinthians 3:18). I do love that word! May God make you love it and feel it. It is a very strong expression. I am afraid that many who use it have not felt the power of it. We *are changed into the same image from glory to glory* (2 Corinthians 3:18). We have the very mind of Christ in us (1 Corinthians 2:16). His graces purify us, His nature adorns us, His law is the rule of our life, and His Spirit is the guide of our conduct.

There is a mine of truth in that text, *In Him we live, and move, and have our being* (Acts 17:28). The image of God is divinely formed in our minds. Don't think you are a Christian because you come here, or go elsewhere, or because you are called a Christian by your neighbors. Examine your Christianity by your Bibles, and remember that the way to do that is to see whether the precious graces of the Spirit of God are to be found dwelling within your hearts and written upon your consciences (Romans 2:15). Let them be rooted and dwell in the soul, and then it will be possible for you to tell that your hearts are under the influence of divine grace.

I am grieved when any bad activity is in my heart, and I desire to go to that sacred sanctifying Spirit who can cleanse and purify the inward inclinations of the mind. What do our earthly doctors do? They ask how our health is. They ask how we feel. They ask what inward complaints we have. They know very well that all complaints arise from within, and if they act wisely, they operate against our inward evils. This is what the Divine Physician of our souls (who knows infinitely more than earthly doctors do) does when He cleanses the very thoughts of our hearts by the inspiration of the Holy Spirit from time to time. It indeed testifies the gospel of the grace of God when such glorious effects are produced on the souls of all those who are true believers in His dear Son.

The apostle Paul here observes, incidentally, that this ministry is from the Lord. Many of us are accustomed to go into the country during the pleasant part of the year. Our first business in the choice of such a place should be to ask whether the church minister preaches the gospel or not. If he does, be thankful and go to hear him. Remember, though, that the preaching of the gospel should be the main thing we should look for in all the public dispensations of Divine Providence. We must remember that unless Christ is preached, we hear nothing. Christ is all in all, and without Him, we are nothing at all.

Paul received his ministry of the Lord; all the ministry is by the grace of God. It is a very strong expression. It pleased the Lord *to testify the gospel of the grace of God*. Those words are very strong in the original. The word "gospel" means glad tidings, good news. There is nothing worthy of the name of good news except that which tells me how it will be with me in a future world. The gospel, properly speaking, and interpreted in its own words, simply means glad tidings. *Behold, I bring you glad tidings of great joy* (Luke 2:10). The original expression is

"This is a gospel of great joy." Where does all this come from? It comes from the grace of Christ.

Oh, I am thankful that grace is in my heart! The same God that gave me repentance must keep me repentant all the days of my life. The same God that taught me to pray will still continue to bless me. The same love that He kindled in my heart must be continually fed by Him so that it may burn up to the glory of His name. The same gracious qualities that His powers inspired must be again and again communicated to the heart so that I may still live agreeably to my profession of faith in Jesus.

The work of the Son is well pleasing to the Father. Yes, with infinite admiration and delight, the Father beholds the glories that dwell in His coequal and coeternal Son. *This is my beloved Son*, said the Father (a fine expression!), *in whom I am well pleased* (Matthew 3:17). We are not able to give the full interpretation of that word. It not only means well pleased, but fully appeased. "I rest in My love; I am well satisfied with it." The delight of heaven is found in the heavenly person of our Lord. And while the Father does delight in His Son, He delights equally to bless all those who are found united to Him by that living faith that the gospel of the grace of God creates in the heart.

These are the principles upon which we may live, and that may testify the power of the gospel of the grace of God upon the soul. It is the divine testimony that God gives to the heart, and I have evidence that I am born again when His blessed Spirit is found to live within me.

This is probably a shorter discourse than I usually give you, but I feel a great degree of weakness this morning, and an increase of cough prevents me from speaking all that I would. However, enough may have been said to reach the conscience of some poor sinner, which may be the cause of his loudest and most ecstatic praises in the world of eternal glory. May the blessing of God be on what you have heard, for His name's sake. Amen.

Chapter 10

His Last Sermon at Surrey Chapel

The last time Rowland Hill occupied the pulpit at Surrey Chapel was nine days before his death. He addressed the teachers of the Southwark Sunday School Society. His tender concern for the welfare of the schools, breathed throughout this address, proves how dear the work was to his heart. It also shows that he could foresee a splendid future for these institutions over which he had watched so long.

Although the reasons for including this address are not based solely upon the quality of the address, we regard it as possessing sufficient merit to justify including it here, especially since it is the last he uttered in public. It is pervaded by that quiet power that was one of the main characteristics of his preaching, and which was due to the sincerity of his purpose, the directness of his intent, and his conscious dependence upon the help and blessing of the Spirit. There is real heart music in this swan song of the venerable pastor, the echoes of which, even at this distant date, may provide counsel and encouragement to the workers in the holy cause.

Prayer before the Address

Oh, hear our prayers, O Lord, that thousands and tens of thousands of celestial blessings may descend upon those who are engaged in this work. They need much of Your Spirit to perform it spiritually. They need much of the simplicity of divine teaching through which they may lead children to begin well in their early days. May they, under Your wisdom, be guided wisely so that they may see the pleasure of the Lord largely and abundantly prosper in their hands.

We thank You for counteracting in some little measure the wickedness of the day by these efforts. We thank You that some who have been teachers themselves have been placed in the ministry of the Word to do much good in the name of Your Holy Child Jesus. We thank You that some who have received this humble education are now preaching the gospel, and that this Sunday school education has been powerfully used to bring many children out of a state of darkness and ignorance who are now leading others to the knowledge of Your truth.

Cause them to prosper more abundantly from time to time. May we all be striving to do the most good, to live more completely for God, and to be fully dedicated to His glory. Bless all other useful institutions. Oh, that we may all lay ourselves out for God and wear well in His celestial service until such time as we are called to enjoy that everlasting rest that remains for Your people in the world of eternal glory. Amen.

An Address to Sunday School Teachers

Delivered at Surrey Chapel
Tuesday Evening, April 2, 1833[15]

If I did not have the highest respect for this important work of bringing up children *in the nurture and admonition of the Lord* (Ephesians 6:4), I could plead my many infirmities as a reason to be silent on this occasion. But if I can only say a little, I thank God for what has already been said to you. In the midst of human weakness, we are satisfied that God can manifest divine power. He speaks, and it is done.

All the work that relates to the salvation of the soul is entirely the work of God. What a wonderful creation is that which I feel within me, and which you all feel, in a bad way or a good one: the existence of the immortal spirit! Every person living will either go in a good way to glory, or in a bad way that leads to everlasting banishment from the presence of God.

Therefore, the instruction of the human mind is of the highest importance. The wisest man who ever lived was undoubtedly the Lord Jesus Christ, who is wisdom itself in the hearts of all His people when He inspires salvation to dwell within them. Second to Him, though, was Solomon, who very wisely says that it is not good for the soul to be without knowledge, or instruction (Proverbs 19:2).

Our good missionaries have gone abroad into many heathen parts of the world, and there they find mankind left totally uninstructed to be monsters of iniquity among themselves. Many are so bad that they will hardly let their fellow beings exist among themselves due to the cruelty of their own savage dispositions.

---

15 Sunday schools were originally schools mainly to educate poor children and to teach them how to read, as these children often spent their weekdays working in factories and in other labor. In addition to providing children with a basic education, these schools also taught the Bible and Christian principles.

In Scripture, the flesh is everywhere mentioned and recorded to be in a most depraved and wretched condition so that it is said that *they that are in the flesh cannot please God* (Romans 8:8). *The carnal mind* is another expression used in the Bible. Though it might not be as plainly worded, it is the same as the fleshly mind, and it is as bad as the devil himself. It is *enmity against God* (Romans 8:7), and nothing worse can be said of human nature, or of any creature, than it is *enmity against God*.

Now what does the gospel propose? Oh, beloved brethren, never forget that glorious truth that is the soul of the Christian religion, and is the Christian religion in the soul: regeneration, being born again of the Spirit, being created anew in Christ Jesus our Lord. Therefore, as my good brother who has been speaking to you has told you already, it is your duty to teach this to children. You who honor me with this visit this evening (for so I call it) as Sunday school teachers should be thankful to God for your privilege. It is my duty, in the midst of my weakness, to address you more urgently.

Oh, my dear brethren, I love you. God bless you, and may He grant that you may live a long time after I am dead to do abundantly more good than I have lived to see done. However this may be, remember that there is no good except that which comes directly from God. Until we are born of the Spirit, it is all darkness; it is all death and hell and sin. You are no more suited for this important duty without the influence of divine grace upon your hearts than a dead man is suited to perform the functions of physical life. If you are instrumental in doing good to others, it must always be from the principle created in you by God having first accomplished that good in your own hearts.

This is why it is to be lamented that while education in general may be looked upon as a blessing, it is literally by no means to be esteemed as a blessing to all. I really do feel, and I think I have too much evidence of it, that in many instances, merely teaching children to read, to go carelessly to a place of worship on a Sunday, while leaving them otherwise uninstructed, is only putting a weapon into their hands that they can never use well until such a time as they are taught by the grace and Spirit of God how to use it. As excellent as Bibles are, they will not convert people except as the spirit and life and power of the Scriptures are brought home to the heart. Otherwise, it is only a dead letter to those who are *dead in trespasses and sins* (Ephesians 2:1).

So then, my dear brethren and sisters (for you may all equally do good), pray particularly for much of the life and power of God to possess your own dear souls. May you be lovely, excellent, and zealous Christians, walking before God in a manner that is well-pleasing in His sight, remembering that as He who has called you is holy, so you are to be holy *in all manner of conversation* and godliness (1 Peter 1:15).

Indeed, you will never desire to do the work of God (except it will be to you as drudgery) until such times as righteous desires are implanted in your hearts by God Himself, by which you will be directed. Just as preachers are not to be content with displaying their ability in presenting a fine sermon in order to gain the admiration of the people, so you will travail with these little children in birth until Christ is formed in them (Galatians 4:19). Then you will be taught to teach them as Christ teaches us all.

While you have these children before your eyes, I think you will feel desirous not only to teach them the letters of the Book, but also the spirit and the meaning of the Book that they are taught to read. I think you will be instructed to understand that it is important for you to especially remember the children of poor parents, and that it is your business to essentially do with them what God has done to you, we trust, spiritually and powerfully – made you to feel the glories of His regenerating grace, and to know what it means by having the blessed experience of the same upon your hearts.

Before us now is the Holy Book. You will be naturally instructed, I believe, to mention to your children the infinite holiness and purity of God in Himself – how He can never look upon sin except with infinite detestation and abhorrence. You should never see the children before you without trying to make them detest and abhor sin too. You should tell them that all their miseries arise from their inward corruptions, and that these must be overcome in them before anything that is good can be truly practiced by them.

I don't merely say this to those who give exhortations to children, but I speak to you all as teachers. While you have your little classes before you, try to teach something of what you know that may be instructive to them, and attempt to have them really see the wickedness, the excessive hideousness of sin. Then lead them to that power whereby alone grace may be implanted to counteract their natural corruption, for we cannot tell how soon grace may begin in a poor child.

Let us praise God that in this Sacred Volume we are told that *out of the mouths of babes and sucklings* God could ordain strength (Psalm 8:2; Matthew 21:16). While the Pharisees in their spite and enmity could cry out against Christ, *Crucify Him, crucify Him* (Luke 23:21), the little children could cry out in the temple and say, *Hosanna to the son of David: Blessed is he that cometh in the name of the Lord* (Matthew 21:9). You cannot tell how soon God begins with the human mind.

Until I considered it more deeply, I thought we were carrying things a little to the extreme by the education of children as young as five years old in schools. I now think quite otherwise. I am very well convinced that we cannot begin teaching too early. The earlier they are brought under the regulations of a Christian education, the better. Yes, it is better indeed for us who are living in the present generation. It is also infinitely better for the children themselves, who are to form the next generation, when that divine knowledge, through the blessing of God on your instruction, has been so communicated to the mind that the fine, glorious passage of wisdom is accomplished in their hearts when they are made in their early days to *abhor that which is evil* and cling to that which is good (Romans 12:9).

From these considerations, my dear brethren, with tenderness of heart and affection for the good of the souls of the children, you will be taught that nothing is done well unless it is done in the spirit of love. *Love is the fulfilling of the law* (Romans 13:10). Love melts, and nothing else but love can melt the hardest heart, the stony heart, and make the heart of stone become a heart of flesh (Ezekiel 36:26). You will dwell on the lovely story of how Christ Jesus came and offered Himself as a sacrifice for sin. You will tell the children, in language they can best understand, the need of being acquainted with the Savior, how they should love Him, and what obligations they are under to obey Him.

Then you will lead them to the instructive part of the Word of God, for that is the second part of the business. First, you teach the child what he is and what he must be before he can be a good child. Then, after he is made a good child, after grace has possessed the heart, you may teach him the practice of goodness – tell him how he should behave himself. You cannot sow good seed in uncultivated ground. Let the ground be first well plowed and broken up.

Oh, God, send down the conviction of sin on the children of the rising generation; then we will do all we can to show, among such little sinners as these are, what grace there is in Christ to change their poor little hearts, and to teach them in their early days to be devoted to the love and service of the living God.

I don't think you do a quarter of the good you otherwise

would do in merely teaching a child to read unless you remember that yours is a Sunday school, and so teach them to read, and to understand what they read, that they may be better for it. It is really amazing that those who are concerned in some of our schools do this in a very clumsy manner. Although I suppose they do as well as they can by teaching what they know from their own miserable selves, it is really sad to see how little profit there is in it. We have our national schools; I pray to God to equip them to teach, but I am told that the children are not much better for going there, but rather worse, going out of the schools as bad as when they went in. In some places, they say they are afraid to send their children to such schools because they get more harm by being associated with bad children than if they did not go at all.

It is a matter of fact that the rising generation will be an extremely corrupted generation – unless the grace of God, that brings salvation, is early imparted to their hearts, teaching them to deny *ungodliness and worldly lusts* (Titus 2:11-12). Faith teaches this, but we don't understand anything about grace except as it is divinely communicated from above. Therefore, see that children are taught to look for this gift so that they may be instructed in those things that relate to their everlasting peace. And though we should not be proud of it, yet we should be thankful for it.

Consider the blessings that frequently result from this. I thank God that we have some (may the Lord make us very humble) people who are now laboring in the ministry of the Word who had their first instruction in our Sunday schools. There are a great number of good people who have got themselves well associated by being connected with good people, and connected constantly with each other, and so they now watch over each other wisely and well. I do not think they can do anything other than live to God since the Lord has honored them by placing them among the honorable family of Sunday school teachers.

Yes, my dear brethren, you are doing an abundance of good, and you do not know what good may yet be done. The more you are filled with the grace of the gospel to teach, the better you will be enabled to do this in a good and spiritual manner. Oh, may the Lord send down upon your dear souls ten million times more of that spirit of wisdom and understanding, that sweetness of divine knowledge, that love to the precious souls of men, and that love toward one another – especially toward the children of the poor. May He give your tongues gracious liberty, and may He teach you that although there is a sacrifice made by serving in these schools, yet the Lord is pleased to make the sacrifice a pleasant one, as your labor *is not in vain in the Lord* (1 Corinthians 15:58).

I remember that a poor man once met me at the corner of the street and showed me a little bit of paper. He asked me, "Will you be so good as to read this for me?"

I said to him, "Can't you read it for yourself?"

He replied, "No, sir. I was not born in the days in which there were many Sunday schools, but my children can read well, and they read to us after I have finished my labor. We were never so happy since we have begun to read Christian books, to look into our Bibles, and to pray that we may be governed by their contents."

May the Lord allow you to have many such instances as this, in causing many families who are hells full of wickedness to be little heavens, by God Himself dwelling in the midst of them, for we live unto God when the Spirit lives in us. Therefore, you will judge that it is in vain to instruct any of the rising generation except as they themselves receive early instruction from God and are taught the necessity of being regenerated and born from above. Indeed, the doctrines of divine grace, though mysterious (*How can these things be?* [John 3:9]), may be explained, and I do not doubt that they will be, in language that young children may be led to understand.

Can you not tell them of the pride and anger of their hearts that is working in them the evils that are produced there? Can they not be told that these evils come from the evil nature within them? Can they not be told how grace can conquer these iniquities, how God can give them early repentance for early sins, and how He can renew their hearts in a wonderful, wise, and gracious manner, even as they are first setting out in life? Praise God that we sometimes have instances set before us of this kind in a remarkable, sweet, and happy manner.

I regret, my dear brethren, that I cannot now serve you as I desire to. My strength is gone, but my heart and affections are where they have always been. I am particularly eager to present this, my last testimony, on behalf of your important duty that you have undertaken in instructing the poor man's child and the present rising generation.

Go on, my dear hearers! May God bless you in every effort! Pray much for His Holy Spirit so that you may have the spirit of eminently wise holiness dwelling in your minds, and that you may be taught how to instruct children in the best of wisdom in their early days. When I look at the foolishness, senselessness, corruption, and sin, I see foolishness in their conduct and beasts and devils in their behavior; but when I look at the children of God, I see the effects of the power of grace in them that is well worthy of that gracious glory that such children are to fill in eternity.

I pray to God that these things may do you all good. I am very sorry that I speak with so much feebleness, but I am glad still, even in this, that in the midst of my declining strength, I feel where my heart is. I cannot give you a finer exhortation to conclude with than that verse, 1 Corinthians 15:58, from which my good young brother has earlier addressed you: *Therefore, my beloved brethren, be you steadfast*: don't be wavering in any part of your duty. *Unmovable*: that will prove that you are steadfast indeed, if there is no moving you from it. We cannot imagine how much we increase in the work of the Lord except as we abound in it. *Always abounding in the work of the Lord.*

Oh, there was a time when preaching to me was not tiresome work. I was very glad to go from town to town and from village to village preaching the gospel to as many as I could. You are young. Use your youth for God and His glory while you have time. Remember that it is in time alone that you are to do good. We can do more good on earth than we will be able to do in heaven. It is done beforehand there. There will be no good to be done in heaven. There will be a good deal of good to receive there, but it is all done. Remember, then, that this is the time to do good.

Here you are amid the enemies of God, and here you may prove His glorious strength. May the blessings of the eternal God be abundantly poured down upon you so that you may always abound in the work of the Lord, and as you have already proved, you will prove that *your labor is not in vain in the Lord*. Many good preachers have already been raised up from Sunday schools. I will not mention some names that I could mention, and for this reason you will say that they were inferior Sunday school boys before they became useful and fruitful ministers of Christ – but that should not deter us either. Some Sunday school teachers have been called from that occupation to the work in which they are now appointed, and which they are honorably filling to the eternal salvation of the souls of many.

May the God of all grace give you all the blessings that you need in the work. I thank you for your kind attendance, and I am sure I have to thank you for your patience and goodwill. Not being able to speak as I could wish, you will accept that which I have now offered to you in the name of our Lord Jesus Christ. May the blessing of God be with you all evermore. Amen.

Other Similar Titles

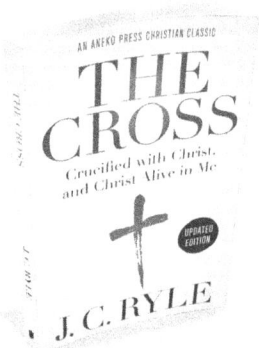

The Cross, by J. C. Ryle

I want to tell you what perhaps the greatest Christian who ever lived (the Apostle Paul) thought of the cross of Christ. Believe me, the cross is one of deepest importance. This is no mere question of controversy; this is not one of those points on which men may agree to differ and feel that differences will not shut them out of heaven. A man must be right on this subject, or he is lost forever. Heaven or hell, happiness or misery, life or death, blessing or cursing in the last day – all hinges on the answer to this question: "What do you think about the cross of Christ?"

Available where books are sold.

Expository Thoughts on the Gospel of John,
by J. C. Ryle

Wisdom, encouragement, and exhortation is contained in these pages. Not because of the author's brilliance, but because of the words of truth contained in the gospel of John. And just as the Apostle John didn't draw any attention to himself, so also J. C. Ryle clearly and wonderfully directs his words and our thoughts towards the inspired words of scripture. If we truly love God, we will love His word; and the more study His word, the more we will love God.

Available where books are sold.

Holiness, by J. C. Ryle

He who wants a correct understanding of holiness must first begin by examining the vast and solemn subject of sin. He must dig down very deep if he wants to build high. Wrong views about holiness are generally traceable to wrong views about human corruption.

Practical holiness and entire self-consecration to God are not given adequate attention by modern Christians. The unsaved sometimes rightly complain that Christians are not as kind and unselfish and good-natured as those who make no profession of faith. Far too many Christians make a verbal proclamation of faith, yet remain unchanged in heart and lifestyle. But Scripture makes it clear that holiness, in its place and proportion, is quite as important as justification. Holiness, without which no one shall see the Lord (Hebrews 12:14). It is imperative that Christians are biblically and truly holy.

Available where books are sold.

Straightforward Thoughts for Young Men,
by J. C. Ryle

Young men, you form a large and very important class in the population of this country; but where, and in what condition, are your souls? I am growing old myself, but there are few things that I can remember so well as the days of my youth. I have a most distinct recollection of the joys and the sorrows, the hopes and the fears, the temptations and the difficulties, the mistaken judgments and the misplaced affections, and the errors and the aspirations which surround and accompany a young man's life. If I can only say something to keep some young man walking in the right way and preserve him from faults and sins, which may hurt his prospects both for time and eternity, I shall be very thankful.

Available where books are sold.

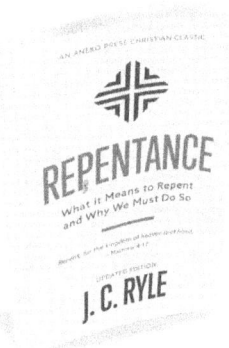

Repentance, by J. C. Ryle

It is indifference that leaves people alone and allows them to go their own way. It is love, tender love, that warns them and raises the cry of alarm. The cry of "Fire! Fire!" at midnight might sometimes rudely, harshly, and unpleasantly startle a person out of his sleep, but who would complain if that cry was the means of saving his life? The words Except you repent, you will all likewise perish might at first seem stern and severe, but they are words of love, and they could be the means of delivering precious souls from hell.

Available where books are sold.

Christian Leaders of the Eighteenth Century, by J. C. Ryle

My purpose in compiling these biographies was to present to the public the lives, characters, and work of the leading ministers whom God used to revive Christianity in England in the eighteenth century. I had long believed that these great men were not sufficiently known, and as a consequence, their value and merit had not been sufficiently recognized. I thought that the church and the world should know something more than they seem to know about such men as Whitefield, Wesley, Romaine, Rowlands, Grimshaw, Berridge, Venn, Toplady, Hervey, Walker, and Fletcher. For twenty years, I waited anxiously for some worthy account of these mighty spiritual heroes. At last I became weary of waiting, and I resolved to take the pen in my own hand and do what I could in the pages of this book.

Available where books are sold.

www.ingramcontent.com/pod-product-compliance
Lightning Source LLC
Chambersburg PA
CBHW070137080526
44586CB00015B/1734